REMEMBERING WRIGHT STREET

Charles Edward White

REMEMBERING WRIGHT STREET
© Copyright 2009 by Charles Edward White

ISBN # 978-0-9840555-5-5

Printed in the United States of America

The Publishing Place
www.thePubPlace.com

REMEMBERING WRIGHT STREET

Life, Love, and Laughs of a City Boy Growing Up in the 1940s and '50s

Charles Edward White

A Note to the Reader

This book is written in a casual, conversational style because I wanted it to read like I was sharing these true stories with you face-to-face. I could've written in the more formal English of textbooks and other such scholarly works, but that style of language didn't suit my purpose. Some chapters will make you laugh; a couple might even cause you to shed a tear. That's O.K. Those were my emotions when I wrote them.

When reading this book, you'll run across an occasional expression or word that was in common use back in the time and place in which the stories are set. If you lived then and there, you'll *know* what they mean. If you didn't, their meaning in most cases will be fairly obvious from the context. If you're still puzzled and *really* want to know, try asking a person who grew up in that era for a definition or explanation. Doing so should bring a smile to their face and you'll make their day. As a last resort, there's always that thing called a dictionary. If none of the above works for you, let me know.

This book contains richly detailed descriptions of certain unforgettable persons, places, and things I knew as a boy. I wanted to enable you, the reader, to visualize them with your mind's eye the way I originally saw them and remember them. My overall goal was to tell these stories in a way that's not only readable, but enjoyable—with a bit of "inspirational" here and there. Did I succeed? See what *you* think.

--C.E.W.

P.S. Your comments and questions are always welcome. Contact me via e-mail at: ~~CandJWhite@PeoplePC.com~~. I look forward to hearing from you.

chuck white57@twc.com

To my father and mother who raised
three children on Wright Street.

Acknowledgments

Special gratitude goes to my sisters, Sandra Lee ("Sandy") White Foster and Jacqueline Sue ("Jackie") White Whitney, who were continuing sources of encouragement and forgotten details while I was writing this book.

I will always be indebted to fellow Manual High School alumni Gordon Durnil (Class of 1954) and Dale Mortenbeck (Class of 1956) for sharing their personal memories and for performing valuable research. They contributed greatly to this book's completeness and accuracy.

Another big thank-you goes to my good friends Shelley Adams, Kay Rugg, and Su Shortridge for reviewing portions of my manuscript and making numerous helpful observations.

And, finally, my deepest appreciation goes to my dear wife, Joyce. Without her ongoing patience and understanding I could never have fulfilled my longtime dream of writing and publishing this book.

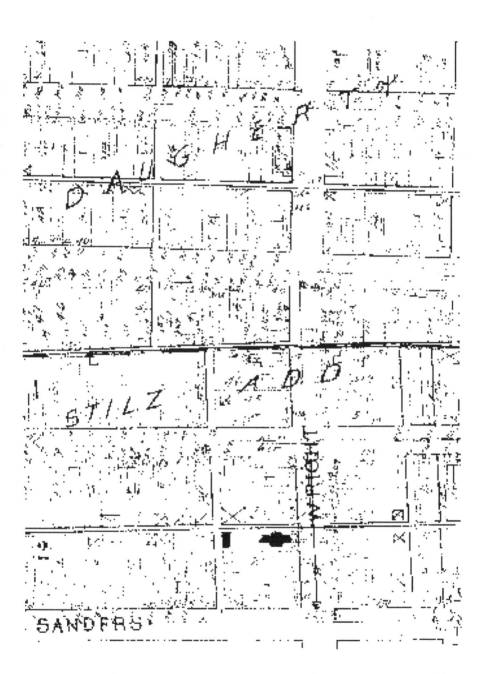

Contents

APPENDICES

Introduction

A Walk Down Wright Street

Ten blocks long and only twenty-four feet wide. Not much of a street by most standards, it was just one of the hundreds of thoroughfares criss-crossing inner city Indianapolis. One thing, however, set this short, narrow street apart from all the others: my family lived on it from the early 1940s until the mid-60s. This was the street where I grew up: Wright Street.

The main stretch of Wright Street—the portion most familiar to me—ran straight north and south from Buchanan Street down to Cottage Avenue. Between these two T-intersections, Wright crossed Woodlawn Avenue; Prospect, Morris, Sanders, and Orange Streets; and Parkway and Terrace Avenues. A short northern extension of Wright Street was offset to the west and ran from Buchanan for one long block north to McCarty Street. A short southern extension was also offset to the west at Cottage and continued one more block south to Weghorst Street. I grew up while living at 1218 Wright in the middle of the block between Morris and Sanders.

1

Wright Street, like most older city streets, was originally surfaced with bricks. Many years before we lived there, these were paved over with asphalt. This stone and tar mixture was notorious for turning soft and oily during the dog days of summer. Tracking that sticky black mess into the house was a mistake you didn't make twice. The four-inch high curbs along Wright Street had been hand-cut from long pieces of Indiana limestone. Since our street was so narrow, parking was allowed only on the west side. This was the side we lived on.

Three-foot wide concrete walks ran along both sides of the street. They had an unusual bumpy surface created by thousands of tiny embedded pebbles. The walks had taken on a gray-brown color over the years, stained by countless fallen leaves lying in puddles of autumn rain. A few sections of the walks had become cracked and pushed upward by large tree roots. Most of us kids skinned our knees more than once as a result of tripping over those cracks while running and playing.

All blocks of houses in our neighborhood had alleyways running through them. These alleys provided access to people's backyard garages. The alleys were also where the city picked up our garbage and trash. Kids frequently rode their bicycles and played basketball in the alleys because there was little or no traffic. The lot we lived on abutted the south side of the alley cutting through our block. This alley was paved with concrete. Many shorter, lesser-traveled ones were left unpaved. People living along those alleys often covered them with cinders from their coal-burning furnaces to help control dust and prevent their dirt surface from turning to mud.

A variety of maples, sycamores, and other trees grew in the yards along both sides of our street. Some of them towered nearly a hundred feet high with trunks so thick you couldn't put your arms around them and touch your fingers together. Of course, my arms were shorter when I was a boy. Still, these were really *huge* trees. In the summer, it was possible to walk in their shade along much of Wright Street. These trees also provided a haven for the neighborhood's numerous gray squirrels.

Wright Street ran through a residential neighborhood. The only businesses were a few small corner groceries. There were five of these mom-and-pop stores along the street's main eight-block length. Having a grocery just a half-block away was really handy. Whenever my mother needed something in a hurry, I could

3

run down to Fisher's Market—because it was the largest and closest—and be back home in less than ten minutes.

Wright Street was closely lined with the modest one- and two-story houses of working-class families like ours. A few of these houses were doubles (side-by-side units) and duplexes (over-and-under units). Home ownership wasn't as common back then. Many of the families in our part of town rented their homes from landlords. We were among those who owned their home. Nearly every house in our neighborhood had a large front porch equipped with either a wooden porch swing or a metal glider. People were out on their porches often in those sweltering Indiana summers before air-conditioning, both to cool off and to socialize.

In our neighborhood, not every family had an automobile and certainly none of them had two. Traffic was, therefore, never a problem along Wright Street. Sometimes, as long as half an hour could pass and not a single car would go by our house. Even so, my two younger sisters, Sandy and Jackie, and I were never allowed by our ever-watchful mother to play in the street. Our main play area was the wide sidewalk in front of our house. Here we enjoyed hours of fun roller skating; riding scooters, trikes, and bikes; pulling each other in our Radio Flyer wagon; and playing jacks, hopscotch, and other outdoor games.

In the mid-1960s, life on Wright Street changed drastically. A vast triangular tract of land on the inner city's southeast side was purchased and cleared for construction of the interchange of Interstates 65 and 70. This wiped out the northern four blocks of Wright (from Buchanan down to Sanders) and cut across many other thoroughfares in the area. The result was a maze of dead ends, rerouted side streets, and a gutted neighborhood. Unfortunately, the house I grew up in was demolished as one of the hundreds doomed because of this massive highway project.

Mom had been a widow for a couple of years by then and all three of us kids had grown up, recently married, and moved out to make our own lives. The new highway right-of-way only partly overlapped our lot, so the state bought my mother's house and front yard, but not her garage and most of the back yard. Mom sold the garage to the neighbors behind our house before she joined the exodus to the suburbs.

The old garage stood alone for thirty more years, but it's gone now. Only the concrete foundation remains as a visible reminder that something once stood on the property at 1218 Wright Street. That rectangular outline serves as a "tombstone" marking one of hundreds of "graves" resulting from the death of a neighborhood. Most of the lots were swallowed whole with nothing left behind to mark their passing.

The coming of the interstate highways brought the end of an era. With half of Wright Street now eliminated and many families relocating, the little grocery stores that remained struggled on for a while, but eventually closed their doors forever. Their closing was also hastened by competition from the large new chain groceries called "supermarkets" that were opening out in the suburbs.

As the older families like ours died off or moved away, a new generation with different values, priorities, and lifestyles moved in. What was left of the old neighborhood began deteriorating. Eventually, it took on a seedy appearance. Those of us who had lived on Wright Street during its golden years hated to see it come to such a sad end. It deserved better. Far better.

The following chapters look back at some of the people, places, and events that I knew and experienced along the street I grew up on a lifetime ago. Within these pages, the tall trees still shade those eight blocks of Wright Street in the summer, people still sit out on their front porches and chat across the railings, American flags still ripple in the breeze at nearly every house, and neighbors still know and genuinely care about one another.

I remember these things because I lived on that street while growing up from a boy of seven into a young man of twenty. Today, thinking back across the years that have slipped by so quickly, I wish everyone could have had the privilege I did of living there. Come with me now and let's go back to the Wright Street of half a century ago . . .

1

Dad and Mom

Most kids at one time or another assume that their parents are the meanest, strictest, and/ or weirdest parents on earth. I had such thoughts at times; but, actually, my folks were fairly typical parents of the World War II and post-war era. Let me tell you about them. My two sisters and I were fortunate to grow up with both our father and mother present in our lives. Dad was kept from military service due to a medical deferment, so he didn't disappear from our life either temporarily or permanently. Many not-so-lucky kids had no fathers at home during the war years; others lost their fathers forever as war casualties.

My father worked as a district circulation manager for one of the three Indianapolis newspapers published in those days. This meant he was responsible for Monday-through-Saturday distribution of *The Indianapolis News* in a certain part of the city. During the war, because of manpower shortages, he managed two districts on the city's southeast side. After the war, he had one district covering the Fountain Square area.

This included Wright Street and the surrounding neighborhood where we lived. After turning twelve, I carried *The News* on a route in Dad's district. Having your father as your manager wasn't easy, but he was fair about it. He didn't expect any more of me than any other carrier; neither did he expect any less.

In addition to his regular job, Dad was also quite an entertainer and loved "show business." He was a ventriloquist and a magician who was proud of his membership in the International Brotherhood of Magicians. Dad was also talented musically. He could play a guitar, harmonica, and violin (or "fiddle" as he called it), as well as sing. Regrettably, I inherited absolutely none of his musical abilities or his flair for showmanship. Dad was considered a professional because he was usually paid for his work, although some was on a volunteer basis. He would say he was an entertainer to earn extra money, but you could tell he got a big kick out of doing it—even if he had never been paid. In any case, he thoroughly enjoyed being in the spotlight in front of a crowd. When I was old enough, I went with Dad to many of his performances and helped carry and set up his equipment. Each of these trips was a real adventure for me.

When Dad wasn't working at his news-paper job, he actively served as a volunteer in the USO during World War II. This organization presented free shows to entertain our military personnel. All the big names went on tours overseas; the lesser-known entertainers like my Dad performed on the home front. Dad always served as the master of ceremonies in the USO shows he was in. He introduced the other entertainers, cut up with the audience between acts, and also performed his magic and ventriloquism.

Dad often performed in shows presented to wounded soldiers recovering at a large military hospital at Camp Atterbury, an Army base several miles south of Indianapolis. Once he took our whole family along with him and my two younger sisters—who were far braver than I was—did a hula dance. I can remember seeing row after row of young men in blue bathrobes and white pajamas. They were laughing and clapping and having a good time. Many of them were in wheelchairs. Some of them were missing arms and legs; others had head and face wounds all wrapped in bandages. I wondered how they could be in such terrible condition and still have so much fun. Dad and the other performers were glad to bring a few minutes of entertainment to these veterans who had sacrificed so much for our country.

Dad stayed really busy earning a living at his regular newspaper job. Any free time was devoted to his USO work and other "show jobs," as he called them. After the war, Dad pursued a secondary career in show business and was quite successful at it. With the right breaks, he could easily have become a somebody in the entertainment world. He went as far as a local and regional entertainer could go, but never made it into the "big time" on the national scene.

Even though Dad didn't read much for personal enjoyment, he used to read the comic strips to my sisters and me every day before we were old enough to read them ourselves. Way back then I can remember thinking that someday I'd be able to read and to understand for myself what those cartoon characters were saying to one another. I still consider his reading to us as children a great motivator that led to my own lifelong love of books.

Dad had no hobbies that I knew of. He never played golf, went hunting or fishing, or followed team sports. The only sport that he enjoyed at all—if you can call it that—was professional wrestling. Dad was a real fan. I don't know if he was a true believer who thought it was all "real" or if he knew it was faked and he just liked the wild action. Whatever the reason, he attended wrestling matches as often as our limited finances and his busy schedule would allow.

Dad also took in an occasional night of boxing, but it never held the same fascination for him that the "rasslers" did. He took me with him to wrestling and boxing matches several times while I was a young boy. I can vaguely remember seeing Gorgeous George, Ali Pasha, Lou Thesz, and other famous wrestlers. But the boxers were all total unknowns to me. I thought the whole idea of grown men beating on each other and acting so crazy was all pretty silly.

When I was old enough to express my total lack of interest, Dad quit taking me to the matches and eventually gave up going himself. I'm sure he missed them, but he never complained. As a result, I grew up with no interest in any sports-related activities, except for my high school's football and basketball games. I went to those regularly to support my school, but it was as more of a social activity than out of any great interest in the games themselves.

My mother was a stay-at-home mom in those days when most moms still were. So she was always there to take care of us. Back then, raising a family was considered a full-time job in itself. Mom hardly ever went to the beauty parlor or worried about having fancy clothes. She didn't wear much make-up except for special occasions, and there weren't many of those.

Mom sewed a lot on her old pedal-type sewing machine, but it was more out of necessity than desire. She made many of her own clothes, as well as for my sisters. She was quite good at it. The girls' outfits always looked nice on them. Mom liked to embroidery in her spare time, what there was of it. She also took an active part in the PTA, as many non-working mothers did in those days, and served in various offices. With three of us in school, Mom was also a room mother for one or the other of us through most of our years attending Horace Mann School #13 and Abraham Lincoln School #18.

Most kids back then walked home from school for lunch; we did, even though we lived about a mile away. Mom had something good to eat ready for us every day. We had to eat in a hurry in order to make it back on time. One winter on an exceptionally cold and snowy day (they didn't cancel school or let it out early as easily back then), my teacher told me just before lunch time not to go home, but to report to the principal's office. I did as directed and there was good old Mom. She had trudged ten blocks through ankle-deep snow in a real central Indiana blizzard to bring my sisters and me our lunch. She also brought us our rubber boots which we hadn't worn that morning before the snow came. Only a truly caring mother would perform such a selfless act of love for her children. Our mother was the *only* one who thought to bring her children their lunch that day. It really made us feel special. She may not have expressed her love verbally as often as some moms, but she certainly demonstrated it time and again by this and other loving acts.

Both our parents worked together to raise us right. They took us to church regularly and instilled biblical values in us. They weren't alone in doing this; many parents in those days did the same. That's one of the main reasons why I still believe that the 1940s and '50s were such a great time to grow up. Looking back, it seems that, in spite of our many wonderful scientific, medical, and other advances, America has gone downhill from where she once was in many of the ways that truly count the most.

As children, my sisters and I may not have had all the things we wanted in life, but Dad and Mom saw to it that we had everything we really needed. And for that we are still grateful today. Our hope is that we have successfully passed on to our children—and they in turn to theirs—the valuable lessons of life our parents taught us while growing up on Wright Street.

Abraham Lincoln School #18 still stands along the south side of Palmer Street between Ringgold Street and Barth Avenue. The building is currently occupied by a church group using it as a community outreach center. The exterior of the building looks exactly as it did in the 1950s; the interior retains much of the original look although a few classrooms have been modified for other uses. The old gymnasium on the top floor (the one that was "off limits" to students in the '50s) has been re-opened and is back in limited use.

2

Wheels: A Brief Personal History

The pages of history don't record the name of the unknown person who created one of the world's greatest inventions: the wheel. Whoever it was, I'm sure had no way of knowing what they were getting started. Since that distant day, mankind has developed and perpetuated a special fascination with wheels and anything that runs on them. While growing up on Wright Street, my life rolled along on a series of wheeled devices. Something new on wheels came into my life at the rate of about once every year or two.

Starting with the day I was born — January 25, 1939 — I rode on wheeled conveyances even before I was consciously aware of them. It's possible, though I have no way of knowing, that my very first ride as a hatchling was when I was transported from the new-baby nursery to my mother's hospital room several times a day in a four-wheeled miniature baby bed. Or, depending on the hospital's practice at the time, I may have simply been carried to her room in the arms of a nurse. So we can't count this for certain as my first wheels.

When my mother and I were discharged from the hospital after several days, I probably rode with her in a wheelchair from her room in the maternity ward down to the hospital lobby. Or maybe one nurse carried me while another pushed Mom in the chair. Since hospitals have never had an overabundance of nurses on staff, most likely I was riding with Mom.

The very first wheels that I know for certain I rode on were those on the 1938 Studebaker Champion that my Dad drove when he brought Mom and me home from Saint Francis' hospital in Beech Grove. They lived on the northeast corner of Wright Street and Sanders Street at the time. This house was across the street and down three houses from where I was destined to live and grow up later at 1218 Wright.

While still a baby, I was taken for walks by my proud mother who pushed me around in a baby buggy (sometimes called a baby carriage). These were the forerunners of the strollers that are so popular today. The buggy was sort of a miniature baby bed on rubber-tired wheels six to eight inches in diameter and had a sturdy handle for pushing and steering. The buggy had a collapsible "convertible top" that could be raised and positioned to keep the sun off the baby. Once again, this was before my ability to remember, so I'm speaking from general knowledge gained much later.

I know from old family photographs — black and white ones with the jaggedy edge around them — that while a toddler I had a Taylor Tot. This unique set of wheels was all-metal (no plastic in those days) and was designed with a detachable foot tray and pushing handle. Mom took me for walks in it after I was old enough to sit up unassisted. As I got a little older and began using my legs, the foot tray was taken off and the handle removed. Then, I could wheel around the house in it on my own like the fancy walkers used today, but without all the bells and whistles. Taylor Tots were popular in their day, but disappeared from use decades ago, along with baby buggies.

My first wheels that I personally had control of were on a tricycle. Since I was only three or four at the time, exact details are unavailable. My knowledge of having one comes, again, primarily from old family photos. I do remember that when I was a few years older my two younger sisters rode a trike that had obviously been around for awhile, so I must have been its original rider. The trike was built of sturdy steel and lasted through all three of us kids. My sisters liked to ride it together. Usually, Sandy would sit in the seat and pedal and Jackie would ride behind her standing on the little platform made for this purpose over the back axle. We all enjoyed countless hours of fun on the trike.

My first set of four wheels that I can clearly remember was a red wagon. By some unwritten rule, all wagons were red in those days. Back then, some kids' wagons, like the famous Radio Flyer, were built mostly of wood and had removable rack panels that made them handy for carrying things. Later, wood was phased out and the wagons became all-metal and had no racks. My wagon was built during the transition period and had a sturdy metal bed. Slots were provided along the sides and in back. Wooden rack panels could be placed in the slots. I'm not sure of the wagon's brand name, it may have been one of the many Flyer models. For some reason, my sisters and I hardly ever used the racks. This was probably because they bounced up out of the slots too easily and were forever falling off. So we just rode around on the wagon bed. It had an unusual rolled edging instead of the usual walled edge common on most wagons then and now.

I usually pulled my sisters up and down the front walk in the wagon, like a big brother was expected to. Sometimes, I'd ride the wagon alone by sitting with my right leg doubled up under me, using my left leg for propulsion, and steering with the wagon tongue. I could get up to a fairly fast speed in this manner. As with all wagons, however, you had to be careful not to cut the front wheels too sharply or the wagon would tip over and out you would go in an instant. I discovered this the hard way a couple of times, fortunately with no injuries other than skinned elbows and knees.

After the wagon, I moved up to a scooter. This was another all-metal toy that ran on just two wheels. I had a deluxe model that came with a brake on the rear wheel. You stepped on a pedal and it rubbed against the rubber part of the wheel to bring the scooter to a stop. After I outgrew the scooter, I don't recall my sisters riding it much, if at all. A scooter was considered more of a boy's toy in our neighborhood.

Next in my parade of wheels was a most unusual riding toy called an Irish Mail. As a boy, I always wondered knew where this thing got its odd name. Long after I grew up, I discovered that it was named after a famous British express train that transported mail from London to Dublin back in the days of steam-powered locomotives. I believe the Irish Mail was manufactured in England, which would explain its unusual name. This four-wheeled, nearly all-metal toy was propelled by pulling back and forth with both hands on a wooden handle connected with linkages to the rear wheels. The front wheels were on pivots and connected together with linkages. The rider's feet were placed on footrests beside each of the front wheels.

The Irish Mail had a very low center-of-gravity, so it wouldn't turn over easily like a wagon if steered too sharply. I found the Irish Mail somewhat difficult to power and to steer. As a result, it was never one of my favorite toys. Another reason why was that some of the kids in our neighborhood made fun of it because they'd never seen one before and thought it looked strange. Actually, it *did* look strange. This didn't make me want to be seen out riding on it. We may have had the only Irish Mail in our neighborhood, but I think that fact was more a source of embarrassment than of pride.

Every kid owned a pair of roller skates when I was growing up. These were not, however, the high-tech multiwheeled inlines popular today. Our four-wheeled skates were all-metal clamp-ons that literally clamped onto the soles of a pair of shoes. Of course, metal wheels running across our bumpy concrete sidewalk made a lot more noise than the silent-running inline skates of today. But we thought making the noise was part of the fun of roller-skating. Every pair of skates came with a special key that was used to tighten and loosen the bolts that controlled the clamps. If you tightened the skate clamps too much, they would warp your shoe soles or, worse yet, tear them loose from the upper part of the shoe. This never made Dad and Mom happy, so we tried to avoid doing it.

On the other hand, if you kept the clamps too loose, the skate would pull away from your shoe sole at the most awkward and unexpected times. Serious falls could result from these mishaps. My sisters or I never suffered any broken bones from our skating falls, but it's a miracle we didn't. We sure had our share of skinned-up limbs. No one wore helmets or protective padding back then. Such things weren't even available. I was never a great skater and thought of skating as something that girls did more than boys.

One summer, all the neighborhood guys my age were building and racing pushcarts. I don't remember how this mania got started, but every boy wanted one. These were simple homemade carts built of whatever materials we could round up. The basic design consisted of about a six-foot length of 2 x 4 — or a 2 x 6, if we could find one — as the main body frame member. Shorter 2 x 4s were attached toward each end to serve as axles. The rear axle was rigidly fastened; the front axle was attached with a large nut and bolt so it could pivot for steering. Wheels were scrounged from whatever source was available: old baby-buggies, wagons, rear wheels from trikes, or similar sources. Since the front wheels didn't have to match the back ones, some pretty odd combinations were used. Whatever worked.

A seat with a backrest often cut from an old wooden chair was attached to the main frame for the driver to sit on. A piece of clothes-line rope was tied on each end of the front axle and used by the driver to steer the cart. Fancier carts even had peck baskets or wooden crates to enclose and protect the driver's legs. When another boy pushed the cart from behind the driver's seat with an old broomstick or piece of metal pipe, these carts would really go at quite a clip. Side-by-side races were held in the alleys to determine who was the "Speed King" of the southside. It wasn't me.

To slow down and eventually stop the cart, the driver had to drag his heels off the front axle. This quickly led to shoes needing reheeling. So, to assist in braking, a hand lever-activated drag brake was usually attached to the frame. These varied in effectiveness. My handbrake was held on with just a big nail. The first time I tried to use it, the whole brake assembly tore loose from the frame and I suddenly had to rely on only "heel power" to stop me.

It's a wonder none of us were seriously injured or killed on these pushcarts, but we all managed to survive — again, without the protection of any helmets or pads.

After several years of riding on three and four-wheel devices, I was ready to graduate to a bicycle. My first bike was a used one with only 24" wheels. I bought it cheap off some kid in the neighborhood. Part of the sales deal was that he would teach me how to ride it. There were no sissy training wheels in those days. You just got on, gritted your teeth, and took off the best you could. My instructions consisted primarily of being told to learn to keep my balance, avoid making sharp turns, and not go too fast at first.

I turned out to be a natural. After wobbling along for a few minutes, I quickly mastered riding, and was soon in my element. Eventually, I got so good that I could ride "no hands" and even learned how to turn corners simply by shifting my weight. I painted the frame black and called my bike "Black Beauty." It came without any fenders or other fancy features, but I loved it. At first, I was limited to riding my bike on the sidewalk. Before long, I was permitted to ride it in the alley beside our house. Finally, I was allowed to ride in the streets. Black Beauty gave me the new freedom and the ability to explore more and more of the Wright Street neighborhood around me.

A couple of years later, I came of age and got what every boy wanted more than anything: a brand-new bicycle. But that's another story.

3

The Amazing Plastic Chicken

Ronnie Morris was one of my best friends during our early years of grade school. He made up for his shorter-than-average height with a bigger-than-average sense of humor. I always enjoyed being around him, no matter what we were doing. Ronnie and his family lived around the corner on — of all streets — *Morris* Street. I thought it was neat that he lived on "his own" street, as if it were actually named after his family. I was "White on Wright," which sounded special because it rhymed; but it wasn't nearly as special as being "Morris on Morris."

The Morrises had four children, all boys: there was Frank, who everyone called Frankie; then, Ronnie; next, there was Byron, known as Buddy; and, finally, there was Pee-Wee. I don't remember ever hearing his given name; he always went by his nickname. Ronnie was fortunate, I thought, to have so many brothers. I envied him because all I had were sisters. They were O.K., but they weren't like having brothers.

One Monday, Ronnie didn't show up for

school. I hadn't seen him that morning like I usually did walking up Wright Street to P.S. #13 and wondered where he was. While taking attendance, our teacher, Mrs. Ault, announced to the class that Ronnie had suffered an attack of something called appendicitis. He was in the hospital recovering from an operation to make him well. After he came home, Ronnie would be missing a whole month of school — that lucky dog. This was back in the days when doctors still thought lots of bed rest was the best follow-up for any kind of surgery.

Ronnie was the most popular kid in our third-grade class; everyone liked him. We were all sorry to hear about his misfortune. Mrs. Ault thought it would be nice for us to make get-well cards to let Ronnie know we missed him and were thinking about him. The whole class agreed that this was a great idea. So we made cards that week during our regular art class time. We each chose our favorite color of construction paper and Mrs. Ault showed us how to fold it like a regular greeting card. Then, we got creative and covered our cards with crayoned artwork and various messages. Some kids used watercolor paints to decorate theirs. Since I lived the closest to Ronnie and we were friends, the teacher appointed me to deliver the cards to him onbehalf of our class.

When I came home from school on Friday, I told Mom what my class had done and showed her the big Manila envelope stuffed with cards that had been entrusted to my care. Mom said, "Since you're such a good friend of Ronnie's, I think you should take them over by yourself and visit him for awhile this afternoon. Don't stay too long and wear him out. Just be home in time for supper. And watch crossing the street going over and back." Our cautious mother was forever reminding my sisters and I to be careful.

I could hardly believe my ears. Mom was allowing me to go solo on my mission to the Morrises'. Getting to go to Ronnie's house was more a journey of trust than of distance. It was only four houses from our place up to the corner of Wright and Morris and another two or three houses across Morris from there. But it was around the corner and out of sight of our house, so I was really getting to go somewhere—and by myself. I felt like my years of good behavior and obedience were finally being recognized and rewarded.

Carefully carrying the envelope of cards, I quickly walked the short distance over to Ronnie's house. Mrs. Morris answered the door and was very pleased to see me. She was a perky little lady with a thick head of black hair flecked with gray. Her round face wore a perpetual smile. Her husband was her opposite in several ways: he was taller, mostly bald, and usually had a more serious look on his face. Mr. Morris had wide-open eyes that didn't seem to blink much. For some reason, he reminded me of the owl in the White Owl cigar ads I'd seen. Maybe this was appropriate because he liked to smoke cigars. My father was a cigarette and pipe smoker, so I'd never experienced the pungent smell of a cigar being puffed until I inhaled it while at the Morrises'. I kind of liked it.

Ronnie was in their living room lying on the couch in his flannel cowboy pajamas. He was surprised by my visit and really glad I came. Right away he wanted to know if I'd like to see his incision. Full of boyhood curiosity, I quickly said, "Sure, lemme see it." He yanked up the tail of his pj top and stretched down the waistband of the bottoms. There just below the right side of his belly was a two-inch incision sewn up with about a dozen stitches of black thread. This was the first surgical incision I'd ever seen. He said I could touch it if I wanted to, so I did. He acted like it really hurt when I touched it, but quickly grinned to let me know he was only kidding.

I asked Ronnie lots of questions about his operation and hospital stay. He wowed me with his answers. Then I told him about Mrs. Ault's surprise announcement to the class and our special art project on his behalf. At this point, I presented him with the big envelope and watched as he opened it. He looked through the two dozen or so cards and read every one out loud to me and his family, who had all gravitated into the living room.

While Ronnie was reading us his cards, my attention wandered over to a brightly colored object sitting on the Morrises' coffee table. After he finished going through the cards, I asked Ronnie, "What's *that* thing?" He said a relative had given him this unusual gift. It was a bright reddish-orange plastic chicken about two and a half inches tall. The chicken—or more specifically, the hen—was filled with white marbles. When the hen's back was pushed down, it would squat, raise its wings, and a marble would pop out of a hole in its butt. The chicken didn't walk or squawk or make clucking sounds; sparks didn't shoot out of its eyes. All it did was lay white marble "eggs." But I laughed every time it did so and thought this was the most amazing toy I'd ever seen. I guess it didn't take as much to amuse kids in those days as it does today.

I emptied the chicken's entire supply of eggs and Ronnie showed me how to reload it. Then, I put the chicken through another round of "egg laying." Ronnie said he had more fun watching my amusement playing with his chicken than he'd had playing with it himself prior to my visit. The novelty must have already worn off for him by the time I came over.

I really liked that silly little egg-laying chicken and was totally fascinated by the mechanism that made it work. Ronnie couldn't help but notice my attraction and offered to give me the toy chicken. I told him that, instead of keeping it, I'd just like to borrow it long enough to take home and show my two sisters. I promised to take good care of it and to return it after Sandy and Jackie had a chance to see it perform. He said O.K.

After visiting with Ronnie and his family for awhile longer, it was getting close to supper time and I needed to get home. Carefully putting the chicken into my jacket pocket, I told Ronnie I'd bring it back tomorrow. He and his parents thanked me for coming over. Mrs. Morris remarked how nice it was that the class had made the cards and sent them to Ronnie. She said she was going to tape them up around the door frame so Ronnie could see them every day while he recovered. She asked me to express his appreciation to Mrs. Ault and all my classmates. I assured her that I would do so on Monday.

As soon as I got home, I couldn't wait to show my sisters the tricky little plastic chicken. I put it through its paces until it was empty. After refilling it, I let each of them take a turn laying a load of eggs. They thought it was kind of clever, but weren't nearly as thrilled with it as I was. When they finished, I just had to have one last round with it before supper. As I pushed down on its back, the chicken got stuck in the squatting position with one wing raised and the other hanging down. Uh-oh. Something in the mechanism inside the chicken had broken and the thing wouldn't work. Now what was I going to do? I had no idea how to fix it, or if it could even be fixed. So, I had to call on a higher power: Dad.

I showed the broken toy to my father, who was handy at fixing just about anything. Dad said he'd never worked on a mechanical plastic chicken before, but he'd see what he could do. He began examining the chicken on top of his desk under the bright light of his fluorescent desk lamp. After unloading the marbles remaining inside the chicken's body, Dad found a tiny piece of broken plastic. He carefully compared one side of the internal mechanism to the other using a small magnifying glass on the end of a letter opener he kept in the desk. Aha! He discovered where the piece had broken off.

Dad told me to go get my tube of model airplane glue which was good for bonding wood or plastic. He couldn't get the short tip of the tube far enough inside the chicken, so he dabbed a drop of glue on the end of a toothpick. After inserting the pick through the egg hole, he quickly deposited the glue on the mechanism where the piece had broken off. Then, using a pair of Mom's eyebrow tweezers, he ever-so-carefully maneuvered the broken-off piece into the chicken's innards and held it in place for a couple of minutes until the glue dried enough to hold it.

We let the chicken set overnight so the repair work could dry completely. Since the next day was Saturday, we got to sleep in later than usual. After we got up and ate breakfast, Dad and I checked his repair job on the chicken. It seemed to work as good as new. The only detectable difference was that the wing on the side where the broken piece had been glued didn't raise quite as high as the wing on the other side.

But this slight imperfection was hardly noticeable. I thanked Dad for coming through for me and fixing the chicken. His repair job only added to his well-earned reputation of being an expert fixer of just about anything—now including broken plastic chickens.

I reloaded the chicken with its eggs and rushed it over to Ronnie's house. I told him the whole truth about how I broke his toy and how my Dad fixed it. Ronnie said it would have been no big deal even if the chicken hadn't been repairable. He said he'd already played with it so much that he really didn't care whether it worked any more or not. I was relieved to hear this, but was still glad that Dad had been able to fix the chicken almost as good as new. I thanked Ronnie for letting me borrow his toy and headed for home.

On the way back, I thought about what I'd learned from this experience: borrowing something from someone—even from a good friend— makes you responsible for it while it's in your care. Whenever I've borrowed anything over the years since then (even though such times have been relatively few), I never fail to remember "The Amazing Plastic Chicken."

4

Johnny Hump

My two sisters and I were good kids, but we weren't perfect. When we disobeyed our parents or did something that displeased them, they had one threat of a punishment so dire that the mere mention of it invariably produced the desired change in our behavior. They—and it was usually Mom more than Dad—would say, "It you don't stop that," or, "If you don't do such and such," then came the scary part that always got our attention and instantly corrected our misbehavior: "Johnny Hump will get you and take you away in his wagon."

This was no made-up boogeyman; Johnny Hump was a *real* person. He was a grizzled old fellow who drove a swaybacked horse pulling a rickety wagon down our alley. We'd see him once a week usually on trash pickup day or the day before. He made his living by picking up odds and ends that people were throwing away. Then, he'd sell what he could to earn a few dollars. Johnny Hump was actually in the recycling business, but back then people just called him a "junkman."

Johnny Hump was not, of course, the man's actual name. Who would have a name like that? This label had been stuck on him by well-meaning, but misguided, parents like ours who used him to scare their kids into obedience. But he really did have a humpback. Maybe it got that way because he was always hunched over as he drove his horse up and down thealleys around our neighborhood.

Every time we saw him, he had on the same tattered brown coat and dirty, gray slouch hat pulled down in the front to hide his eyes. Once I checked him over carefully from a distance with the official Roy Rogers binoculars I'd gotten for Christmas. He looked like he needed a bath, a shave, and a haircut. Overall, old Johnny Hump had the mysterious appearance of someone who actually might haul children away. At least we kids thought so.

Johnny Hump's beat-up wagon had wooden-spoked wheels with steel bands around their rims. It was easy to hear him coming by the grinding noise his wagon's wheels made on the concrete alley. The sound of the hooves of his old nag of a horse slowly clopping its way along the pavement provided further warning of his approach. Believe me, the girls and I made ourselves scarce whenever we saw or heard Johnny Hump coming.

When the weather was nice and we were playing out in the yard, we'd immediately run inside and watch out the window as Johnny Hump rattled and clanked by in his wagon full of junk and scrap metal. We wouldn't go back out until he was a "safe" distance down the alley past our house. As with most kids, it was exciting and fun to be scared a little once in awhile. If our mother was nearby at such times, she might reinforce our fright by saying, "Here comes Johnny Hump to take away some bad children who didn't mind their parents." Is it any wonder we were afraid of him?

We'd peek out from behind the curtains to see if we could spot any cages of misbehaving children he was carting away to do heaven knows what to. We didn't know if he *ate* the bad children; chopped them up and fed them to his big, mean dogs—the ones we imagined he must have—or if he put the children to work toiling in endless piles of junk as his slaves in some secret dungeon. Our Mom never really supplied us with such gruesome details. After all, she was our mother and didn't want to scare us too badly. Our collective young minds created far worse scenarios than she ever could have come up with.

As my sisters and I grew older and realized that we never actually saw any children being hauled off by Johnny Hump, the invoking of his name gradually lost its power. We considered him less and less of a real threat. Eventually, our mother's words of warning about him almost became a family joke. We may not have laughed about it, but we certainly overcame our fears of being taken away to an uncertain fate.

Finally, we realized one day that we hadn't seen or heard Johnny Hump go down our alley for several weeks. We never saw him again. Once or twice we thought we heard the ominous sound of his rattly wagon and clopping horse approaching. But no, we must have been hearing things. Johnny Hump, along with our childhood fear of him, was gone forever.

5

A Christmas Mystery

The Rexall Pharmacy calendar on our kitchen wall reminded me every day in December that Christmas 1949 was getting closer—as if I needed reminding. While I normally would have been ecstatic about the approach of the best holiday in the year, this time around I almost dreaded it. Why? Because my young mind was in turmoil. In less than two months I would turn ten, and my developing powers of reason were struggling with what I thought were some unanswerable questions. As a result, I was on the verge of abandoning my belief in Santa Claus. My growing doubts were a secret I kept to myself, however, since my two younger sisters were still true believers.

I had reached the point where I could no longer believe that Santa Claus—as great and wonderful as he supposedly was—could actually visit every home on earth in one night. How could he possibly carry enough toys with him in a sleigh to fulfill the Christmas wishes of every good boy and girl in the world? And don't forget, he also had to carry enough coal to leave a lump for each child who had been bad. That alone would surely weigh a ton. How Santa came down chimneys presented other puzzling problems. What about apartments that had no individual chimneys? Or houses with chimneys too small to accommodate his famous girth? Or homes like ours where the chimney led directly into a furnace? Wouldn't Santa be trapped inside and burn up?

Out of desperation, I finally shared these bothersome questions with my father. Dad always amazed us kids with his ability to answer any question we could think of, no matter what the subject. He told me that Santa Claus didn't always have to come down the chimney because he had a "magic key" that could unlock every door. I didn't know where Dad came up with that magic key story, but it made a lot of sense to the inquiring mind of an almost ten-year-old. As a result, most of my doubts—but not all of them—went on hold for the time being.

The days of December passed slowly until at last it was that "night of all nights." I joined my sisters in hanging our glitter-encrusted, ornamental Christmas stockings from the mantel of our phony fireplace. Dad and Mom set up this corrugated cardboard contraption—second in importance only to our family Christmas tree—every year as part of our holiday decorations. The fireplace was such an obvious fake that it wouldn't fool anyone, especially not Santa Claus. I guess it was the symbolism that counted. Anyway, I went along with this Christmas Eve ritual mostly to please my parents. But I was no dummy. Just in case Santa *was* real, I still wanted to share in his generosity.

Dad performed his annual reading of "'Twas the Night Before Christmas," we said our prayers, kissed him and Mom good night, and climbed into our beds. We may have been snug, but no "visions of sugarplums" danced in our heads—at least not in mine. Instead, I lay there awake and alone in my upstairs bedroom for maybe an hour struggling with the remnants of my skepticism. Despite my spinning mind, I eventually drifted off to dreamland.

After what seemed like no time at all, I opened my eyes and realized it was Christmas. As I lay there yawning, I looked over toward my bedroom window. A halo of light around the window shade told me that this morning was unusually bright for some reason. Several tiny beams of brilliant light penetrated the semi-darkness of my room through pinholes in the old, worn blind. Each beam illuminated a miniature galaxy of dust particles suspended in the air. After lying there half a minute in total fascination at this unusual sight, I reluctantly climbed out of my warm bed, shuffled over to the window, and raised the shade.

A wonderful sight met my eyes. The most beautiful "white Christmas" I've ever seen lay before me like a winter scene from an old-time greeting card. Everything was covered with a thick blanket of the purest, whitest snow imaginable. Dazzling sunlight blazed from an azure sky and made the snow sparkle like it was sprinkled with diamond dust. I didn't remember snow being forecast; but, somehow, there it was.

As I lowered my eyes and squinted to avoid the intense glare, I spotted something strange on the snow-covered roof of our rumpus room directly beneath my window. Two parallel grooves about four feet apart ran from one edge of the roof to the other. Scattered here and there on either side of the two lines were many small oval indentations in the snow. "Omigosh!" I mouthed half-aloud. But, wait a minute; was I seeing things that weren't really there? After rubbing the sleepy bugs from my eyes, I looked again. The mysterious markings were still on the roof only a few feet away from where I stood.

Just to be sure the marks were not some freak reflections off the window pane, I raised the sash and leaned out for a better look. The icy-cold air stung my face and my breath gushed out in a visible fog as I scanned the roof. Yes, the marks were definitely there in the snow. Questions began rising in my mind. Was it possible? Could the lines really be sleigh runner tracks? Could the other marks be . . . reindeer hoofprints? This was weird. Really weird. Unbelievably weird. My mind wrestled with the thought that perhaps I'd been wrong in my doubting. Whether he had a magic key or not, maybe there was a Santa Claus after all. Right before my eyes was what looked to me like hard evidence of his existence. Who or what else could have made those imprints in the snow?

I was quite certain that my father hadn't gotten out our ladder and crawled up on a slippery, snowy roof in the middle of the night and made all those marks just to perpetuate a childhood belief in my mind. If he had, it would have required that he cross over the back porch roof in order to reach the rumpus room roof. The snow on the porch roof was pristine; there wasn't a mark on it. No, these imprints below my bedroom window were definitely *not* a contrived deception. I looked upward and from side to side, but there were no utility wires or tree limbs overhead or near the roof. Nothing could have dropped accumulated snow to make such markings. There was no "natural" explanation for them.

After thinking about it for several more seconds, the idea burst into my mind that I must share this marvelous discovery. Without even taking time to close the window, I turned and flew down the stairs, recklessly taking two steps at a time. It was so early that my sisters were just getting up and my parents were still in bed. My great excitement made them all think something was wrong, so I quickly assured them this was not the case. Then I insisted that everyone immediately come up to my room and see something amazing. I didn't tell them what it was; I didn't have to. The girls caught my enthusiasm and we raced up the stairway with our house slippers slapping against the wooden steps. Dad and Mom followed us as fast as they could at a more careful pace.

We all crowded around my still-open window. Before my father could ask me why I had opened it in the middle of winter, I motioned toward the roof below and said, "Look!" At first, they thought I was just sharing my window's view of the unexpected snowfall; they didn't notice what I was pointing at. So, I said, "No, look down on the roof!" Four pairs of now wide-open eyes followed my pointing finger.

There was a collective gasp as they all saw what I'd already seen and was so excited about. My sisters leaned out the window together for a better look. They immediately recognized what the imprints in the snow surely must be. While the girls were oohing and aahing and chattering away, I saw my folks look at each other and smile. Dad then confirmed that these markings were indeed positive proof that there really was a Santa Claus—just like he and our mother had been telling us for years.

While Mom was adding her words of agreement, Dad looked over at me and winked. Any remaining traces of doubt vanished from my mind and I became solidly reconvinced that Santa Claus was real. How could I deny it when faced with visible evidence that, sometime in the night, he had landed his sleigh on the roof of our house? As a result of this stunning real-ization, I remained a true believer for one more Christmas. I've lived now for nearly sixty more Christmases since that most unforgettable one. As each December 25th comes and goes, I still wonder: What *did* cause those strange markings in the snow that we gazed at in awe from my bedroom window on that magical morning back when I was a boy? It will forever remain a Christmas mystery.

6

Flag Boys

Even though I never served in the armed forces, I've had a long and strong love for the American flag. One reason for this is that I grew up during World War II. During those childhood years, the flag was flown at nearly every house along Wright Street on most days, not just on certain holidays. People were generally more patriotic back then and wanted to fly the flag to show their support for our country in time of war.

Another reason why I love the flag is because I was a flag boy while in the sixth grade at P.S. #13, Horace Mann School, on Buchanan Street. There were two of us; the other boy was Dick Foster. Because of our shared experience, he became my best buddy from then on through high school. And it all started with us being flag boys together. I'm not sure, but there may have been a third flag boy in case either of us missed school for any reason. If there was such an alternate, I don't remember who he was because neither Dick nor I ever missed being there and performing our duty.

Serving as one of our school's flag boys was quite an honor. Only older boys from the fifth and sixth grades at Horace Mann were eligible. I'm not sure what the exact qualifications were for appointment to this position, but they likely included getting good grades and never causing any trouble in the classroom. Our teacher, Miss Wykoski, nominated us. No doubt she did so because of our exemplary scholastics and behavior.

Two flag boys were required to serve as a team. While one worked the flagpole rope, the other handled the flag and made certain that no part of it ever touched the ground. This was a strict taboo that we were told never to break and it helped instill in us great respect—almost reverence—for the red, white, and blue.

If the flag was damp when taken down, we'd take it to the teacher's lounge and hang it over the backs of some chairs to dry. If during heating season, we'd hang it on a couple of nails in the wall over a radiator. We were never to fold the flag until it was completely dry. Otherwise, it might become soiled by mold or ruined by rot.

After the flag was lowered, we had to fold it exactly in a very precise way. The folding process required that one of us stand at each end of the flag with a corner in each hand. The flag was first folded lengthwise down the middle. Then it was folded lengthwise again, making sure the blue field of 48 stars (remember, Alaska and Hawaii had not yet become states) was showing. After this, the boy on the end opposite the blue field would turn the end of the folded flag up into a triangle and repeat this over and over. After doing so several times, he ended up holding a triangular bundle with nothing showing except the field of stars. The remaining end was then tucked into the bundle to produce a neatly folded flag that, supposedly, looked like an old-fashioned cocked hat like those worn back in the Revolutionary War days. At least that's what we were told by Mrs. Rentschler, the principal, when she instructed us in the details of flag etiquette.

The flag was stored in an unusual place that few of the other students even knew existed. Just inside and to the right of the main entrance into the school was a short door under the back of the stairs going up to the second floor. It looked like it might be a closet door, but it wasn't. This door opened to reveal a steep stairway (actually, more like a ladder). At the top of these stairs, a wooden box was mounted on the left wall. The folded flag was kept in this box. The stairs went down into a shallow cellar under the ground floor of the school building. Dick and I were told *not* to go down these steps; so, of course, what did we do? After resisting temptation for several days, we gave in and went down the forbidden stairway for a quick look around.

Dick went first while I kept watch at the doorway. When it was my turn and I'd reached the bottom of the stairs, Dick closed the access door on me as a joke. I nearly panicked and yelled up for him to open the door. He quickly did so, laughing as only he could laugh. I didn't think it was funny.

Neither of us strayed far from the bottom of the stairs during our visit to this forbidden area. All we could see in the dim light from the windows in the main entrance double doors near the stairs were some old desks and other castoff items. The cellar had a dirt floor, was dark, cobwebby, smelled musty, and was really scary. We never dared to explore this vast netherworld beneath the school beyond this one brief excursion to satisfy our curiosity.

The worst time I can remember serving as a flag boy was one wintry day. Indianapolis had been hit by a freezing rain the night before. As a result, that morning we found the flagpole rope frozen to the pole and coated with ice. Both Dick and I had worn gloves that day, but they were made of wool and we couldn't get a good grip on the icy rope. Out of desperation, we removed our gloves and took turns breaking the rope loose and unwinding it from the cleat near the base of the pole. Then we took turns yanking and yanking on the rope to try and break it free from the pole.

After achieving that, we faced the problem of hoisting the flag with an ice-covered rope. We frantically banged the rope against the pole over and over. Some pieces of ice broke off, but the rope remained stiff and thick and wouldn't go through the pulley at the top of the pole despite our frantic efforts.

We must have lost track of time because Mrs. Rentschler finally came out to check on why we hadn't reported to class. She saw what we were doing and was afraid we might break the rope. So she told us to stop, and thanked us for our efforts. Under such difficult circumstances we couldn't fly the flag that day. We felt like we failed in our duty, even though we had tried our best. By the time we went inside, our bare hands were numb and turning blue from handling the icy rope. I could hardly use my fingers for several minutes. They couldn't have been far from becoming frostbitten.

On another memorable day, after lowering the flag, folding it, and putting it away, I felt an urgent need to pee. A clever idea came to mind that would save me the long walk—or run—out to the restrooms. School #13 was so old that modern toilet facilities hadn't been added until years after the school was built. They were located, along with the steam heating system boilers, in a separate building a good distance behind the school (probably where old-fashioned outhouses had once stood way before our time). I told Dick what I was going to do, so he kept watch outside the door at the top of the stairs.

My physical need overcame my mental dread of the spooky cellar. I descended the stairs, quickly unzipped, and peed into the dirt a short distance away from the bottom step. After obtaining much-needed relief, I kicked some dry dirt over the damp spot to hide it from potential discovery. No one ever went down into the cellar except the school custodians, and they went only on rare occasions. So my little misdeed was never discovered; it remained a dark secret between Dick and me. Not ratting on each other was part of being pals.

Even though we took our job very seriously, being a flag boy had some enjoyable moments. Occasionally, one of us would cut loose and swing from the flagpole rope in a big arc around the base of the pole in a brief moment of boyish fun. Dick liked to do this more than I did; I was too afraid that we would get caught. Luckily, we never did. If the rope had snapped, we could have been injured and would have had some real explaining to do. But ten-year-olds never worried about such things.

We flag boys had to be especially alert on cloudy days. If it started raining, Dick and I were automatically excused from our second-floor classroom to hurriedly go bring in the flag before it got wet. These were the only times anyone was allowed to run in the hallways of the school building. Later, if the rain stopped and the sun returned, we had to go back out and re-raise the flag. Sometimes, this occurred more than once during the day. That was O.K. with us. Getting to leave class, dash through the halls, and thunder down the wooden stairway to the first floor made us the envy of all the other boys. We gloried in our privilege and thought we were something really special. Hey, we *were* special. We were the flag boys.

Horace Mann School #13 (built in 1873) is still standing

on its original location at what once was 714 Buchanan Street (now an interchange of I-65 and I-70) and is listed on the National Register of Historic Places. The building's exterior has been renovated to its original condition; the interior has been remodeled into modern condominiums. The old flagpole still stands at the corner of Noble and Buchanan.

7

My Famous Rope Trick

My sisters and I were really excited. It was the Fourth of July and our parents had invited our neighbors, the Lyons family, over for a backyard get-together. They lived just two doors up Wright Street and had five kids, all about our ages. We played together often and the prospect of spending a whole afternoon in fun and games with them was a happy one.

The Lyonses arrived with their brood at the appointed hour. My sisters, Sandy and Jackie, and I wasted no time in having fun with their kids. While we were playing, our parents relaxed under the trees in the comfort of their wood-and-canvas lawn chairs. As they talked, they enjoyed some "adult" beverages. We kids each got our choice of several flavors of NeHi that Dad had iced down in an old metal washtub. This soft drink was a favorite with children back then because of its bright colors and intense flavors. The tall bottles also held more than the dinky little six-ounce Coca-Colas favored by some people. When we were kids, we couldn't drink a pop whenever we wanted one; it was a treat reserved only for special occasions. As a result, we really looked forward to times like these when we could enjoy a big bottle of cold pop. Orange was my favorite flavor.

After downing our pops and getting charged up from their sugar content, someone came up with the idea to play tag. We quickly decided on some ground rules: no tag-backs, the whole backyard would be open territory, and the back wall of our house would be the "safety zone". Touching this wall meant you were safe from being tagged. With the rules settled, all eight of us kids were raring to get started.

One of the Lyons boys — I think it was Jimmy — volunteered to be "it" and was out to tag anyone he could. My main tactic while playing tag was staying out of the way and avoiding being chased. Eventually, however, Jimmy spotted me at the far end of the yard near the garage. Here he came, so I went running toward the safety zone.

Our house had a back porch with a shed-type roof supported by four round wooden pillars. My Dad had tied a strong rope between the two of the posts for Mom to use as a clothesline. Her main clotheslines were down in the basement so they'd be close to our "modern" wringer-type washing machine. We didn't have a clothes dryer in those days. In the summer, Mom used the line on the porch to hang out her dishtowels and other items. Unfortunately for me, the back porch clothesline was tied just about neck high on a kid my age.

As Jimmy chased me toward the back of our house, I headed between the two pillars holding the clothesline—but I was too absorbed in the chase to see it or to even think about it being there. As I ran, I looked back over my right shoulder to see if Jimmy was gaining on me. He was, but I thought I could make it to the wall of the house and to safety. Just as I turned my head back toward the house, I passed between the porch pillars like a racehorse crossing the finish line. THUNNNK!—I'll never forget that sound. Instantly, my feet flew up into the air in front of me and I fell flat on my back. At first I didn't know what had happened; it was like I'd hit some invisible barrier. I'd run smack into the clothesline at full speed. Fortunately, the back of my head hit on the relatively soft ground as the rest of my body landed on the hard brick porch floor. I wasn't knocked out, but I saw stars for a few moments.

Everyone ran over and gathered around in a circle to see if I was all right. I was a little woozy for awhile and sure didn't feel like any more running or chasing for the rest of the day. Jimmy was sorry about what happened, but it really wasn't his fault. As soon as he saw I was O.K., Dad quickly untied the clothesline from the porch pillars and announced that there'd be no more playing tag. I was the only kid who was in complete agreement with his decree.

The next day, Dad moved the rope up higher on the porch posts so there was no possibility of anyone repeating my crazy little stunt. I think he felt especially bad about this incident because he was the one who had unthinkingly created the hazard. And, like most accidents waiting to happen, this one *did* happen.

I ended up with a real nasty rope burn across my throat and I was darn lucky I didn't break my neck or fracture my skull. After a few days, most of the soreness went away. The ugly red streak I wore on my neck for a couple of weeks or so was a thing of wonder among the kids in our neighborhood. Everyone — even several adults — who saw it asked me about it and looked at it in amazement. A few of my more daring friends even wanted to touch it. I acted like it was really sore when they did, but it wasn't actually that bad.

Eventually, the mark on my throat disappeared completely. When it did, my status of being a neighborhood celebrity also changed; I went back to being just another kid on the block. So ended my brief moment of glory on Wright Street. I have to admit that I kind of liked all the attention while it lasted, even though I earned it the hard way. And, believe me, I mean the *really* hard way.

8

Of Mules and Men

Indianapolis was a major city even back when I was growing up in the 1940s and '50s. Modern improvements from the east and west coasts may have taken awhile to make their way over to this Midwestern metropolis, but sooner or later most made it. "The Crossroads of America" was not, however, a powerhouse of progress in certain areas. In fact, it was way, way behind the times.

One such area was the City Sanitation Department's method of collecting trash and garbage. When I was a boy, Indianapolis hadn't yet converted to modern trucks for making weekly pickups. Instead, the city was still using open hopper-type wagons pulled by teams of mules. That's right, *mules* — those long-eared half-relatives of the horse specially bred for heavy pulling.

About six blocks from my house, the city maintained a long, brick building over on Sanders Street where many dozens of mules were stabled. The pickup wagons were also garaged at this facility and a blacksmith shop was located on the grounds. I can remember sometimes walking by and hearing the metallic clang of the smith's hammer striking against the anvil as he made horseshoes, or in this case they were technically mule shoes.

All the sanitation workers were Negroes (as African-Americans were called in those days). Five men worked on each crew: the mule driver, who got to ride on the wagon, and four can dumpers, who walked along two on a side. Sometimes these men would be singing as they worked together. When they came down the alley on pickup day, it looked and sounded like a scene from the Old South—except that it wasn't cotton in those wagons.

Each wagon had a heavy steel frame supporting a twelve-foot long metal hopper with a deep V-shaped cross-section. The hopper had pivots on both ends so it could be tipped over to one side to dump out its contents. A metal frame ran above the hopper along its entire length. The frame held rolled-up canvas flaps that could be unfurled and tied down to hide the sight of the trash or garbage on its way to the city dump. But there was no way to hide the terrible smell. The wagons were equipped with only one modern feature; they had rubber tires which made them roll along smoothly.

Each wagon was pulled by a pair of two big dark-brown mules. We could hear them coming by the clopping noise of their metal shoes on the concrete surface of our alley. This sound was accompanied by the repetitive banging of metal trash and garbage cans on the sides of the hoppers as the burly black men emptied them.

When we kids were out playing and saw one of the City Sanitation wagons coming, we'd keep on playing if it was the trash wagon. If it was the garbage wagon, however, we ran inside to get away from the horrible stink and from the swarm of flies that usually followed it. In the summertime, you can't even imagine the odor emanating from those open garbage wagons — it nearly took your breath away. After we went in and told our Mom, she would hurriedly close the windows along the alley side of the house to help keep out the odor. How those men on the garbage wagon crews were able to stand it was beyond us. If any government employees ever earned their wages it was them.

One exceptionally hot day, it was about time for the wagons to come by. Mom surprised us while we were playing on the back porch by bringing out her largest pitcher filled with ice water and a bunch of aluminum tumblers. We thought it was for us, but she said no and that we were going to give the trash and garbage men, and their mules, something to drink. She told me to hurry and get our old galvanized metal mop bucket from the pantry, rinse it out good with the hose, and fill it with water for the mules. I ran inside, got the bucket, and did as she directed.

The trash wagon came by first. It always did, so they could stay ahead of the smell of the garbage wagon following about a block behind. As the trash wagon rolled down the alley beside our house, my sister, Sandy, and I took a tumbler full of water in each hand out through the side gate. Our younger sister, Jackie, followed us carrying just one. Mom stayed on the porch and let us kids do the serving. We held the tumblers up and said, "Want some cold water?" Did they ever! The driver pulled the mules up to an instant halt when he heard our offer. The men eagerly gulped the water down and Mom provided refills for any who wanted more. One man handed a tumbler up to the driver. Another man drank his, asked for more, and poured it over his head to cool off.

By this time I'd brought over the bucket and said, "Here's some water for your mules." The driver set the brake, tied off the reins, and jumped down from his seat. He said the mules sure would appreciate the water as much as he and the other men. He held the bucket up for the first mule, which finished off the water in less than a minute. I quickly refilled the bucket from the hose which I'd pulled out to the gate. The second mule also quickly downed a bucketful. While they were drinking, I noticed that both mules were wearing old straw hats with holes cut in the brims for their long ears to stick through. We'd never seen such a sight before. None of the other mules we ever saw wore hats; the driver must have supplied them especially for his team. After the mules finished, the men all thanked us, waved good-by, and continued down the alley banging cans in the afternoon sun.

As you might expect, we weren't as excited about doing the same for the crew of the garbage wagon. Mom told us that those men would be just as thirsty as the ones we'd already given water to. In a few minutes, here they came. We held our breath as long as we possibly could and, then, breathed through our mouths so we wouldn't smell the stink as much. We tried not to let it show, but the men knew what we were doing and just smiled or chuckled about it. The garbage men were all as thankful for the water as the trash men had been, maybe even more so because they realized that providing it wasn't easy for us. I never saw so many flies in my life!

Thanks to our mother's act of kindness that day and her involving us in it, my sisters and I learned an important lesson: thirsty people appreciate a drink of cold water on a hot day no matter what the color of their skin. We could also see that those hardworking men sweating in the sun had a special dignity about them, even though we may not have fully understood at our age what dignity was. They performed a basic, but essential, service to thecommunity even in dumping heavy cans of trash and garbage into open wagons pulled by mules. Indianapolis eventually replaced these outmoded conveyances with modern trucks. Most of the sanitation workers kept their jobs, but the sound of their singing was gone along with the clopping of mule shoes in the alley beside our house on Wright Street.

The City Sanitation Department garage and stables on Sanders Street were razed several years ago and replaced in 1995 with a new facility and parking area for the Indianapolis Metropolitan Police Department's South District Headquarters.

9

David and Goliath

A few cicadas were screeching monotonously high in the trees along Wright Street. It was one of those August summer afternoons when you didn't have to do anything to sweat, and it was so hot that you didn't feel like doing much of anything anyway. My two sisters and I were out on our screened-in front porch. I was sitting on the glider leafing through the slick pages of a big picture book from the library showing what the surfaces of the planets and their moons might look like. Sandy and Jackie were playing house with their dolls and, thankfully, leaving me alone while I explored the wonders of the solar system.

Though deeply absorbed in the book's artwork, I became aware that something had attracted my sisters' attention. Looking up the street, I immediately saw what it was. A little boy we didn't know, maybe three years old, was standing out on the sidewalk in front of the Kesterson's duplex. This was really out of the ordinary. A child that young wasn't normally ever allowed outside alone. And there was something else even more unusual about him: he was wearing *no* pants, *no* underwear, *no* diaper. All he had on was a short T-shirt that barely came to his waist. My sisters were pointing and snickering about this unexpected spectacle. I guess they'd never seen a half-naked boy in public before, at least not one with his *bottom* half exposed for all to see.

Being eleven and the oldest of the three, I was elected by my sisters to become the hero of the hour and go rescue the bare-butted boy from harm's way. Fortunately, Wright Street was not heavily traveled, so the danger was more potential than immediate. No one else seemed to be around. Somebody had to do something. And that someone was me. I left our porch, crossed the street, and walked down to confront Little Mister No Pants.

As I approached the little boy, conflicting thoughts ran through my mind. I, like my sisters, was somewhat amused by his appearance. On the other hand, I knew he shouldn't be out there and I was concerned about doing the right thing. He saw me coming and just stood there staring at me as I came closer. I walked up to him, looked down, and said in my most authoritative eleven-year-old voice, "Your mommy wouldn't want you to be out here by yourself.

You might get hit by a car. You'd better go back inside."

Instead of immediately scampering back into his house upon hearing my wise words of advice, he drew both hands into little fists and rested them on his hips. Then, while looking up at me with his head cocked to one side and one eye squinting in a menacing manner, he said gruffly, "You lemme lone or me *pee* on you!"

His words hit me as unexpectedly and solidly as David's stone struck Goliath. I quickly decided he meant what he said. Not wanting to give him a chance to back up his threat with action, I quickly retreated. After reaching the safety of our porch, I turned around and saw that the boy had disappeared.

"Where'd he go?" I asked my sisters.

"Oh, he went back inside that house he was standing in front of," said Sandy. "What did you say to him?" she asked. Clearly, she was under the impression that he must have gone in because of what I'd said.

"I just told him that his mother wouldn't want him out there and that he might get hit by a car if he didn't go back inside," I replied. My words sounded so brave.

Then came the dreaded question I sensed was coming, but hoped would not be asked.

"What did he say back to you?" asked Jackie.

After a long pause during which I struggled with whether or not to tell them the whole truth, I decided to confess. I always blushed easily and my cheeks reddened with embarrassment as I mumbled, "He, uh, told me that if I didn't leave him alone he would pee on me." Another long pause ensued while I swallowed and tried to think of what else—anything—I could say in my defense. Finally, I blurted, "And I think he really meant it."

They just stood there looking at me for a moment in silence. Sandy looked over at Jackie; Jackie looked back at Sandy. Then, they burst out laughing hysterically. As you can imagine, I did *not* share their amusement. After all, I was only trying to do the right thing. And this was the thanks I got?

Our mother must have heard the girls' laughter and came out on the porch to see what we were up to. "What's so funny, girls?" she innocently asked. Of course, they proceeded to tell her the whole story of how the would-be Hero of Wright Street had been foiled by a mere three-year-old with no weapons other than a few threatening words and a one-inch wee-wee.

I could tell that Mom wanted to join in

with the girls in their laughter, but she held it back for my sake. Instead, she attempted to console me by saying that at least I'd tried to do the right thing. And the little boy had gone back inside after I spoke to him. Maybe I really was a bit of a hero that day on Wright Street. I'll always think so.

10

Cruel and Unusual Punishment?

While growing up on Wright Street, my two younger sisters and I were generally well-behaved children. Like most kids, however, there were times when we bent or broke the rules. When we did, our parents had various punishments to fit the degree of our disobedience. These came in two types: nonphysical and physical (spankings). The *nonphysical* forms of punishment for less-serious offenses included: being sent to our room for a certain period of time, being denied the privilege of going out to play, and standing in the corner facing the walls for a specified time. The various degrees of *physical* punishments escalated in severity from the yardstick, to the razor strap, to the infamous "peach tree tonic" (I'll explain this one in detail later.)

I can remember being sent to my room several times as a boy. But this was no big deal to me because my room was one of my favorite places to spend time anyway. When we were sent to our room, however, it also meant having to lie on our bed during the period of confinement. We couldn't be up playing or doing things—not even reading (although I was able to cheat on this restriction more than once because my bedroom was upstairs and I could hear either of my parents come up the stairway in plenty of time to hide the evidence). This gave us time to reflect on our misdeed and added to the punitive nature of this form of nonphysical punishment. The same was true for standing in the corner and denial of our outdoor play privileges.

The physical punishments were for major infractions of our parents' rules. These disciplinings were applied with the stick, the strap, or the switch. The yardstick was used for the least serious of these violations. The stick was most often wielded by our mother. She would usually take us into the bathroom, make us pull down our pants (or pull up their skirts in the case of my sisters), lower our underwear, bend over, and lean with our hands on top of the toilet seat. Then, she would give us several whacks across our butt. The number given was purely at her discretion; three seemed to be her favorite number. If our misdeed warranted immediate, on-the-spot punishment, Mom might spank us with her hand through our clothing in whatever room we happened to be at the time. These spankings were hardly felt, however, in comparison with the ones administered to our bare bottoms.

Once Mom actually broke a yardstick across my hind end — not because she struck me any harder than usual, but because she must have held the stick too close to the end and it snapped. When it broke on the first whack, I made the mistake of snickering about it. She heard me and was quick to say, "So, you think that's funny do you?" As a consequence, she gave me that whack again, plus three more, with the broken piece and with renewed vigor. Ouch! I never again laughed during a spanking.

If the seriousness of our misbehavior demanded a greater degree of punishment, Mom would say, "You're going to get the strap when your father gets home." We then got to spend the rest of the day in dread of that awful consequence. We would hope and pray that when Dad came home he hadn't had a bad day because the strength of his application of the strap seemed to be in direct proportion to how he was feeling at the time he applied it.

Most kids and many adults today don't even know what a razor strap is. Back in our day, most men shaved with so-called safety razors that used replaceable blades. Electric razors were available, but hadn't really caught on yet. Unfortunately, we had an old-fashioned father who used neither of these types of modern razors. He used what was called a straight razor. Barbers and hair stylists still use them today for certain types of hair cuts.

Straight razors required regular sharpening, or honing, by repeatedly dragging the edge of the blade back and forth across a rectangular piece of flat stone called a whetstone. Then, to remove any burrs or rough spots from its edge, the blade was rubbed several times up and down a razor strap. This was a piece of heavy leather a little less than a quarter of an inch thick, about three inches wide, and maybe a yard long. Dad kept his strap hanging on the back of the bathroom door. This was a convenient location for use with his razor and also for use in administering punishment. I don't remember Dad using the strap on my sisters (except maybe once or twice on Sandy), but he sure used it on me several times. And I deserved every one of them.

"Getting the strap" involved meeting our father in the bathroom, closing both doors, pulling down your pants (but not your underwear), bending over and placing your hands on the toilet lid, gritting your teeth, and closing your eyes. Right before strapping me, Dad would always ask, "What have you got to say for yourself?" This was the time for an admission of guilt by saying that I understood what I had done was wrong. Next, Dad would ask, "Are you sorry you did that?" I'd answer, "Yes, sir." He would then ask me, "Are you ever going to do that again? I'd answer emphatically, "No, sir!" Then, Dad would utter those words that every child has heard in these situations, "Now, remember, this is going to hurt me more than it is you." I couldn't really understand what he meant, or believe what he said at the time. Years later, after becoming a father myself, I understood. I even said the same thing to my three sons before spanking them. They were lucky. I used an electric shaver, so had no razor strap for use in their punishment.

As with the yardstick, the number of whacks given with the strap depended on the whacker; the whackee had to receive them without further comment or excuse. Any attempt at argument would only be rewarded with one or more additional whacks. I learned that if I yelled out loudly on the first whack, it seemed to lessen the force of application of those following. I'm sure the sound of my voice carried well beyond the bathroom walls to the listening ears of my two sisters. So, even though the misdeed and the punishment were mine, they learned a lesson from it as well. And that lesson was: don't make the mistake of doing what I did — *it's not worth it!*

Finally, there was the worst physical punishment of all, the one we dreaded the most: peach tree tonic. This quaint name was what my father's father had called it when he administered it to my Dad back when he was a boy. I never understood why Dad called it peach tree tonic when we didn't even have a peach tree, but I never dared to ask him why. This type of punishment was administered only for the most grievous infractions. I remember receiving it just once — and, believe me, once was enough.

Receiving peach tree tonic required going out into the backyard and finding a thin, green, pliable switch from one of our trees. If none was on the ground, one had to be broken off the tree. The switch had to be just the right length to satisfy my father, about two feet long. Then, all the leaves were carefully removed by the one being punished. I don't know exactly what kind of trees we had in our yard. Whatever kind they were, they had perfect branches for this unusual use. How unlucky for me.

I remember getting and preparing the twig, which added to the misery of the total experience. I handed the instrument of punishment to my Dad. He swished it through the air a couple of times to ensure that it was sufficiently flexible. That unforgettable sound was a foretaste of what was coming. I don't even remember today what my misbehavior was. It was likely an outburst of smart-mouthed back talk. Neither of our parents would ever tolerate sass from any of us kids. Anyway, whatever I had done so infuriated my father that he applied that switch right there in the yard. He didn't make me bare my posterior since we were outside. I was wearing shorts at the time, so he switched me across the back of my upper legs. I still remember that I got five lashes and how I "danced" while I was receiving them — talk about something stinging. I ended up with long, red welts across my legs; they were sore for days. Those marks made a strong physical impression on me and an unforgettable visible impression on my sisters. They never had to experience this level of punishment. Lucky them.

I don't believe that my sisters or I ever really hated our father or mother for disciplining us with physical punishment. If we did, such thoughts were short lived. We grew up realizing and accepting that they loved us and were doing their duty as good parents to teach us right from wrong. An important part of their teaching was that punishment is an inevitable consequence of disobedience to those in positions of authority. As a result, we grew us respecting our parents, our teachers, the police, and adults in general. In other words, *all* authority figures—right up to and including God Almighty himself.

I wish more modern-day children were brought up experiencing strong parental discipline administered in love, so they could learn a similar lesson. Unfortunately, over concern for the possible abuse of the few has been allowed to outweigh the far greater need for the training of the many. The lack of disciplinary punishment in the home and in our schools has resulted in a multitude of problems plaguing today's society. The times were far different back when we were kids on Wright Street. Even though our butts may have occasionally been sore for awhile as children, we all grew up into responsible adults. And for that we can be thankful for having a father and mother who didn't "spare the rod."

11

Leo

Scrape, scrape. Scrape, scrape. Scrape, scrape. Scrape, scrape. People living along Wright Street knew what this strange sound meant whenever they heard it: Leo was coming. He could be heard from half a block away as he scraped his way along the pebble-textured sidewalks. Scrape, scrape. Scrape, scrape. Scrape, scrape. Scrape, scrape.

The scraping sound was made by thick chunks of steel attached to the heels and soles of Leo's black leather, high-top shoes. The steel pieces helped keep his shoes from wearing out as a result of the unusual way in which he got himself around. He "walked" by balling up his fists, swinging his arms out in wide horizontal arcs, leaning forward, and twisting his upper body from side to side at the waist. He literally had to drag his legs along beneath him. They were both bent outward at the knee, so that only the steel pieces on the inner edges of his shoes actually contacted the sidewalk.

Leo was the only person I'd ever seen with legs bent like this. As a naturally curious eleven-year-old, I asked my mother what was wrong with him. She told me and my two younger sisters that Leo had a disease called polio when he was young and it left him crippled. We may not have understood exactly what polio was, but we knew for certain that we sure didn't want to get it and end up like poor Leo.

Leo was always dressed in a pair of heavy trousers, a long-sleeved shirt with a little black leather bow tie, a buttoned-up vest, and a flat wool cap. Even in the hottest part of the summer, he wore the same outfit, but would leave off his tie, roll his sleeves up above the elbow, and unbutton his vest. Leo was probably in his forties and had salt-and-pepper hair, black bushy eyebrows, and prominent front teeth. He also had weak eyes and wore round, steel-rimmed glasses with thick lenses. There was one other thing about Leo: he was smiling most of the time.

Whenever Leo passed anyone on the sidewalk, or if they were in their yard or out on their porch, he always spoke. If he had the time — and he usually did — he would stop and chat for a few minutes with the adults while catching his breath. He seemed to know everyone's name; he even knew mine. People in our neighborhood were polite to Leo. Some of the younger children may have been a little afraid of him because he was "different," but no one ever called him names or made fun of him.

We didn't know exactly where Leo lived; it was somewhere a few blocks up from our house on one of the side streets crossing Wright. Common knowledge around the neighborhood said that Leo lived with his widowed mother, who was in poor health, and that he was all the family she had.

Once in a while, Leo would pull a small, obviously homemade, wagon behind him by a piece of rope tied around his waist. The wagon was made from an old wooden crate and what looked like used baby buggy wheels. He would be headed to Fisher's Market down on the corner of Wright and Sanders. Since Leo couldn't carry bags of groceries in his arms while walking in his own peculiar way, he used the wagon. Fisher's provided free delivery service, but Leo prided himself in bringing his own groceries home.

At other times when Leo went down the street without his wagon, I wasn't sure where he was headed or why. He may have been going to collect from the customers on his newspaper route. Yes, even with his handicap, Leo got out every morning before dawn and delivered *The Indianapolis Star*. He used his wagon to go get his papers from the pickup station because they weren't dropped off at carrier's homes, as they are today. Then, he had to pull that wagon full of heavy newspapers several blocks to his route and deliver them seven days a week, no matter what the weather. Collecting for the paper each week was especially challenging for Leo. Most houses had steps up to their front door; climbing them was very difficult for him. Somehow, he managed.

One summer day while out washing my bicycle, I heard a voice faintly calling for help. I turned off the hose, walked down the side of our house toward the street, and rounded the corner of the porch. Across the front yard, I spotted Leo lying on his back in our hedge. He had evidently crossed the alley that ran beside our house and fallen while stepping up on the curb. His pant legs had slid up above his ankles and I could see something I'd never noticed before: Leo had metal braces on both his legs.

There was a gash on Leo's forehead where he fell against one of the hedge's stiff branches. His glasses were lying nearby on the sidewalk; they were bent, but not broken. I tried my best to pull him up out of the thick hedge. Leo was not a fat person, but he was much heavier than a skinny kid like me. And he couldn't help himself because of his legs. After my vain solo rescue attempt, Leo said to hurry and find someone to help me pull him out.

I ran inside the house and got my mother. Together, we pulled and pulled on Leo's arms until he finally came out of the hedge and was sitting upright on the sidewalk. Mom rushed back in to get some first aid items for his cut which, luckily, was small and not too deep. After she finished bandaging Leo's forehead, I handed him his twisted glasses. He fiddled with them until they were more or less straightened back into their original shape. After trying them on and making another minor adjustment, he seemed satisfied.

Since Leo was sweating profusely, Mom asked him if he would like a drink of water. He said he would, so she sent me in to bring him one. I brought out the biggest tumbler I could find filled with cold water from the glass jug we kept in our Frigidaire. Between gulps of water, Leo thanked us again and again for helping him and apologized repeatedly for damaging our hedge. Mom told him not to worry because we could easily straighten the branches back into position. During those few minutes we spent together, it was obvious even to an eleven-year-old that Leo was greatly embarrassed by what had happened.

After drinking all the water and declining our offer of more, Leo sat there for several minutes fanning himself with his cap. He wiped sweat from his face and neck with a big bandanna that was always hanging out of his vest pocket. When he finally felt ready, we helped him struggle up onto his feet. This proved even more difficult than pulling him out of the hedge. Once he was standing, Mom asked Leo if he needed any help getting where he was going, but he said no, he would be all right.

Leo stood there for a few more seconds getting his bearings. He thanked us both one last time, smiled, and patted me on the shoulder in a gesture of appreciation. Then, swinging his arms and twisting his body, he went on his way down Wright Street. He was a little slower than usual at first, but soon got up to his normal pace. Scrape, scrape. Scrape, scrape. Scrape, scrape. Scrape, scrape. We watched him until he was over a block away and we were sure he was doing O.K. I heard Mom say quietly, half to herself, half to me, "Poor Leo." Then, she went back inside.

Standing there a few moments longer watching him scraping his way on down the street, I can still remember wondering why someone with legs so badly deformed would make the extreme effort required to get from place to place. I thought that if it were me, I would probably just stay in the house all the time feeling sorry for myself and never go anywhere. But Leo didn't let polio and crippled legs stop him. He went where he needed to go and did what he needed to do without a trace of self-pity. And always with a smile and a friendly word for everyone.

In a way, Leo was like his glasses that day he fell in our hedge. He was bent, but not broken. Without ever knowing it, Leo taught the people in our neighborhood a valuable lesson about living with what we all considered a severe physical handicap. As I grow older and face life's inevitable infirmities, I hope I never forget that lesson or Leo, the special man who taught it so well.

12

Real Horsepower

During my childhood years, our neighborhood was served by two large dairies: Roberts Dairy and the Polk Milk Company. My family was a Roberts customer. Roberts delivered their milk and related products to your door from shiny trucks driven by friendly neighborhood milkmen. Polk, on the other hand, had not kept up with the times. They still made their home deliveries using milk *wagons* pulled by *horses*.

Our Roberts milkman would drive up in his cream-colored truck wearing a clean, white uniform complete with a black-billed, military-style cap. His competitor came clip-clopping up Wright Street in a mustard yellow, box-shaped, enclosed wagon pulled by a brown horse. The Polk milkman wore a dull gray uniform and cap that looked rather dinghy in comparison with that of the Roberts man.

The Polk milkman had one—and only one—advantage over his competitor. Every time the Roberts man delivered to a house or two, he had to return to his truck. He would carry

91

back the empty glass milk bottles he'd collected from his customers' milkboxes and pick up more full bottles in the metal tote he carried. He had to keep moving his truck up the street every few minutes. The Polk man could deliver to a couple of houses and, then, call his horse by making a certain clucking sound in the side of his mouth. The horse was so well trained that it would come up the street to the milkman and save him a lot of trips back to the wagon — the wagon literally came to him.

I don't know if all Polk's horses were trained like this one on the Wright Street route or not. Maybe this horse and driver had developed a special working relationship over the years. If all their horses were trained to do this, maybe that's one reason Polk kept using them instead of trucks. Polk's management must have thought that horses were more efficient and time-saving.

The Polk wagon was equipped with a covered bucket and a flat-bottom shovel. If the horse pooped in the street, the Polk milkman had to stop his deliveries and scoop up the mess. I guess it was considered bad for public relations if one of their horses "did its business" in the street. The wagon also carried a canvas feedbag full of oats which allowed the horse to eat lunch while pulling the wagon along the milk route.

The Polk company logo was a life-size cow's head painted prominently on the sides of their wagons. The head was enclosed in a large circle around which ran their slogan: Polk's Milk – Always Ahead. While this was a clever play on words, I wondered how they considered themselves "ahead" in any sense of the word when they were still using horse-drawn wagons to deliver milk in the early 1950s. The only modern feature of the Polk wagon was that it ran on automobile-type rubber tires.

Polk finally started upgrading from horses and wagons to trucks, but by then it was too late. They'd already lost so many customers that they went bankrupt. I don't know what they did with all those horses. The poor things probably ended their years of faithful service by being sold to a dog food company or to the proverbial glue factory.

Roberts Dairy must have felt good about coming out on top in their long-time competition with Polk. Their victory, however, was short-lived. A chain of new dairy stores opened up around the city and consumer buying habits were changing. The big new supermarkets taking the place of the small neighborhood groceries also offered large selections of fresh milk and dairy products at attractive prices. All this competition put Roberts out of business in another year or two. Even their shiny trucks and spiffy uniformscouldn't save them — they were doomed. The days of door-to-door milk delivery were over.

I found out after writing this chapter that the Mutual Milk Co. was another dairy serving Indianapolis, but don't remember seeing them make deliveries in our neighborhood.

13

Through the Window Glass

Dad and Mom weren't home. He'd taken her on a quick shopping trip. Since Mom never learned how to drive (lots of women didn't back then) Dad always took her anywhere she needed to go. In any case, our Grandmother White was visiting for a few days and she was keeping an eye on us while our parents were gone. Or, I should say, she was *supposed* to be watching us.

Grandma was a wiry little lady barely five feet tall. She was probably only in her 60s at the time, but we kids thought she was "really old." Her once coal-black hair had a few wisps of gray and was always done up in a knot at the back of her head. We never saw her in anything but dresses and black leather lace-up shoes with thick two-inch heels. No matter what the season, she always wore a heavy cardigan over her dress. I think she suffered from what they used to call "poor circulation." Grandma was from a tiny rural community called Stilesville in the next county west of Indianapolis. As a long-time widow, she was used to a quiet, stress-free life alone. No doubt coming to the big city and watching three rambunctious kids like us was a real challenge for her.

After our folks left, Grandma sat down in the living room and leafed through a magazine for several minutes. Before long, she laid her head back on the chair and nodded off as she usually did late in the afternoon. Sandy, Jackie, and I tiptoed out to the rumpus room at the back of our house and closed the door so we wouldn't wake her. We thought it was really something that we were on our own for awhile.

Lacking anything better to do, we decided to play tag. Not just regular tag, but a new version I came up with. As with any game of tag, we had to designate what would be our safety zones. And it was my bright idea that safety would be anything made of glass. In other words, if the person who was "it" came after you and you touched glass you were safe from being tagged. I named our new version of the old tagging game "Glass Tag." Wasn't that clever?

I started off being "it" and quickly tagged Sandy. Jackie and I then began darting around the small room, twisting and turning to avoid being tagged. We were all laughing and having a good time, but tried to keep the noise down by shushing each other so we wouldn't disturb Grandma. Sandy made a swipe at me and barely missed as I jumped away from her. My left arm was outstretched in an attempt to touch the window in our back door so I'd be safe. My palm and fingers were held flat and at an angle to my wrist, like when a policeman holds up his hand to signal "stop." I must have lunged toward the window with more force than I realized.

To my complete amazement, my entire hand and wrist went right through the window glass—*without even cutting or scratching me.* I didn't feel a thing. Unfortunately, the big oval-shaped hole I broke out of the window pane had a long spear of glass jutting up from the bottom. After pushing my hand through the glass without injury, the weight of my arm caused my hand to drop. The point of the glass spear then penetrated at least an inch into the underside of my wrist.

Instantly, we weren't laughing anymore. We all froze where we stood. I used my other hand to slowly lift my wrist up off the glass spear point on which it was impaled and ever-so-carefully pulled my left hand through the hole in the window. Blood—*my* blood—was on the glass, running down my arm, and dripping onto the floor in front of the door. It's a wonder

I didn't pass out, but I remained conscious. As I slowly turned my wrist over, I didn't want to look. When I did, I saw a one-inch by one-inch triangular flap of skin hanging down from a nasty looking V-shaped cut. This was obviously not the usual stick-a-band aid-on-it type injury. It was way beyond that.

My sisters started yelling for Grandma. She woke up, hurried out into the rumpus room at her fastest granny speed, and went into a near frenzy. She grabbed me by my good wrist and pulled me through the kitchen and down the hallway to the bathroom. All the while my cut-open wrist was dripping a trail of blood spots the size of nickels across the linoleum floors. The girls were both crying because I was hurt and bleeding. Strangely, instead of being concerned about my injury—which actually didn't even hurt—my main thoughts during these panicky first minutes were more on how I was really going to "get the strap" for this little escapade.

When we arrived at the bathroom, Grandma didn't know what to do. All she could think of was to run cold water on my wound. I vividly remember hanging over the edge of the sink and watching my blood swirling and swirling and swirling in the water as it spiraled down the drain. I didn't know much about the human body at my age, but I knew enough to realize that it had a limited quantity of blood. I wondered how long I'd bleed before I ran out.

In a totally detached way, I looked down into that opening in my wrist and could clearly see one of my forearm bones and the artery running beside it. I thought it was pretty neat to look inside my own body. Fortunately, the glass had stabbed into me at an angle and had just missed the major blood vessel or I wouldn't be here to tell about it today.

At this point, my parents arrived home to find the kind of total chaos that every parent dreads: my sisters bawling, blood everywhere, Grandma in a tizzy, and me slowly, but surely, bleeding to death into the bathroom sink. Between sobs, my sisters quickly told Dad and Mom what had happened. Working together, my folks quickly took control of the situation. Mom carefully pushed the flap of skin closed on my wrist and wrapped my wound tightly with many layers from a roll of gauze. This didn't totally stop the bleeding, but slowed it down considerably. I was beginning to get a little weak in the legs by then from all the blood I'd lost. Mom could tell I was getting woozy and had me sit on the toilet lid so I wouldn't fall over.

Dad got on the phone right away and

called our family doctor to see if he was still in his office. By this time, it was after five o'clock and his regular office hours were over. The phone rang and rang until someone finally picked it up—it was the doctor. He asked Dad a few questions and said to bring me in and he'd wait for us. Mom wrapped a bath towel around my wrist and hand for added protection and off we went. The girls told me good-by with a look on their faces like they'd never see me again. I hoped they were wrong.

After a slower-than-usual trip down Shelby Street because of rush hour traffic, we arrived at the office of Dr. Charles Reid near Garfield Park. His nurse had already left for the day, so he tended to me unassisted. Dr. Reid looked a lot like Peale's famous painting of George Washington, except that he was bald. The doctor's look, voice, and demeanor were all very reassuring to a scared kid like me with a hole in his wrist the size of a pop bottle cap.

Dr. Reid didn't waste any time getting right to work on me. First, he carefully un-wrapped the gauze Mom had wound around my wrist. When he saw the size of my wound, he asked me how I'd managed to cut myself so badly. I told him about how we were playing Glass Tag and my hand went through the win-

100

dow glass. He was not impressed. In fact, he made a comment about that sounding like a pretty dumb game for kids to play. He was right, of course. Next, he cleaned and disinfected my wound with a liquid of some kind (it may have been iodine). Whatever it was, it burned like fire. He fanned it with his hand to make it evaporate and quit stinging; I tried to help by blowing on it. That darn antiseptic was more painful than the cut itself.

The doctor then had me lie down on the examination table and cranked up the part behind my back so I could see what he was doing. I watched in an odd combination of fear and fascination as he injected me in several spots with a numbing agent. Then, he began stitching up my wrist with what looked like plain black thread. I could feel the tug of the suture material as he pulled strands of it through my skin. My being sewn up didn't really hurt, but it sure felt weird. By the time he finished the ninth stitch, I'd seen about all I wanted to see. Finally, the repair job was done; the flap of skin was neatly stitched back into place. While applying a bandage and placing my arm in a sling, Dr. Reid complimented me on taking it all so bravely (he meant because I hadn't cried like a big baby). In fact, I never shed a tear during the entire ordeal although I sure came awfully close when he applied that iodine.

Dr. Reid checked my records and found that I'd received a tetanus shot within the past year, so I avoided getting poked again. Before we left, he gave my parents and me some verbal instructions on how to follow up. He also wrote a prescription for the universal cure-all: penicillin tablets. These were just in case my wound started showing any signs of infection. It never did, by the way. Maybe Grandma's improvised cold-water flushing procedure washed out all the germs. More likely that stinging iodine burned them out.

After we returned home and my parents had more time to think about what had happened, they became very upset. They were angry with the three of us for being so unruly while we were in Grandma's care, for thinking up and playing something as dangerous as Glass Tag, and for breaking the back door window. On top of all this, didn't we realize I could have *died* if that glass had cut my artery? No, we obviously hadn't thought about such things in our childish pursuit of some innocent fun. Later, another sobering question crossed my mind. If Grandma didn't know what to do for badly cut skin, how would she have coped with a severed artery spurting blood? I still shudder to think about the probable answer to that question.

Dad and Mom must have been so relieved that I hadn't died and was going to be all right that they had mercy on me and my sisters. As a result, we weren't punished and got off with a stern warning that any similar acts in the future would result in our getting the razor strap for sure. Believe me, we never played Glass Tag again. To this day, the V-shaped scar on my left wrist still reminds me that I am VERY lucky to be alive after my close call with death that scary day on Wright Street.

The small stone building that housed Dr. Reid's office is still standing at 2445 Shelby Street. It is currently serving as the office of an income tax preparation service.

14

Kissed by Hedy Lamarr

An odd structure stood at the corner of Wright and Sanders, three doors down from where I grew up. This two-story, box-shaped apartment building with six units seemed out of place among all the smaller houses around it. People moved in and out of these apartments with far greater frequency than most of the families renting single houses or half doubles in the neighborhood. I sensed that my parents—especially my mother—eyed "the big house" with a certain amount of suspicion. In my childhood innocence I had no idea why.

One summer day while my sisters and I were playing out on the front walk, I noticed a boy about my age sitting on a concrete step beside the big house. I'd never seen him before and figured he must have recently moved into one of the apartments. While riding my bike up and down the half-block I passed him a few times. He finally looked up from the comic book he was reading, smiled, waved, and said "Hi." I said "Hi" back.

After completing another circuit on my

bike, I decided to stop and talk to the boy. This wasn't like me; I'd always been on the shy side. But I figured he probably didn't know anyone since he was obviously the proverbial new kid on the block. He told me his name was Drake Phillips, but everyone called him Junior. He said he liked that nickname better than Drake which was kind of an unusual name. Junior was a year older and a little taller than me. He was one of the few boys I ever knew who had blonde hair. Junior said I was the only kid in the neighborhood he'd met since he and his mother had moved in the previous weekend. They must have done it on Sunday while we were gone to church because we hadn't even noticed the apartment had changed hands.

Junior and I hit it off immediately. We talked for quite awhile on the step outside his apartment and quickly discovered that we shared a love of action-type comic books, especially *Superman* and *Captain Marvel*. It was really hot out in the sun, so he invited me to come inside and see his giant collection of comics. My sisters and I weren't allowed to just disappear off the sidewalk and go into someone's house without asking our parent's permission. I told Junior I'd be right back after I ran home and rounded up my own modest collection of comics. Actually, I went home to get Mom's O.K. to go inside his house. I hoped that she'd be agreeable with my request.

My mother was busy in the kitchen peeling potatoes for supper. I told her about meeting the new boy, our mutual love of comic books, and his inviting me in to look at his. "Can I, Mom?" I asked. "Please. It's just down at the corner." She was hesitant at first. "Charles, we don't even know those people. I don't want you going into strangers' houses." I didn't know what she was afraid of. So, I pleaded, "Mom, I'm almost twelve. Shouldn't I get to do some things that I couldn't do when I was younger?" While she was thinking that one over for several seconds, I also assured her that Junior seemed like a nice kid. I stood there silently with a hopeful look on my face. My tactic must have worked. Finally, after finishing the potato she was working on, she relented and gave her permission. She also reminded me not to stay over an hour and to "mind my manners." I said O.K. and thanked her. I grabbed my comic books from their storage box on the sun porch and headed out the door.

I quickly walked down the street to Junior's place. After I knocked on the screen door, he swung it open and said, "Come on in."

The sun's brightness outside made the interior seem really dark at first. Once inside, I noticed their living room window shades were pulled down all the way. The blinds had seen better days, but managed to keep out most of the sun. An oscillating fan on a table over in the corner was trying its best, but all it could do was blow the hot air back and forth. After my eyes adjusted to the semidarkness, I could see that the living room furniture looked a little rundown and the carpet had several worn spots. But I didn't care about things like that.

Junior said he wanted me to meet his mom. I plopped down on the sofa while he went into another room to get her. In a few seconds, he returned with a woman I couldn't believe was his mother. She looked young enough to be his older sister. Her long dark-brown hair was perfectly styled. Her facial makeup accented her big brown eyes and she had the reddest lips I'd ever seen. She was wearing a yellow satin robe tied tightly at the waist. This accented her curvaceous body. She smiled and said "Hello. I'm Junior's mother."

She sure didn't look like anyone's mother I'd ever seen. She was beyond cute, beyond pretty, even beyond beautiful. She was absolutely *gorgeous* — what they called a real "knockout." Junior's mom was also a dead ringer for a popular movie star of the day named Hedy Lamarr. I don't mean that she reminded me of Miss Lamarr, or that she kind of looked like her — *she could have been her twin sister*. If the actress had for some unknown reason dropped out of the Hollywood scene and changed her identity, she could have been Junior's mother. And something told me that she was well aware of her great similarity to the movie star and maybe even enhanced it by the way she wore her hair and makeup.

I sat there with my mouth hanging open for an awkward moment or two. Then, remembering my manners, I stood up and said, "I'm pleased to meet you, ma'am." At least, I think that's what I said. I looked over at Junior. He had a great big grin on his face like he'd seen this kind of reaction before. Junior's mom told me to sit down. She sat herself in one of the overstuffed chairs and crossed her legs. As she did, her robe parted enough to reveal them both from her knees down. I may have been only "eleven-and-a-half-going-on-twelve" at the time, but I was enthralled. Suddenly, I was interested in looking at something other than comic books.

After a few minutes, Mrs. Phillips asked

us if we'd like something cold to drink. That sure sounded good. So, we both said we would. She got up and sashayed out to their kitchen. While she was gone, I said to Junior, "Gosh, your Mom sure is pretty. She looks like a movie star." He said, "Yeah, I've heard that before." Mrs. Phillips soon came back with three bottles of Coca-Cola. This was a real treat since my family usually only enjoyed soft drinks on special occasions. Boy! I thought I was in heaven.

As the three of us sat there in the sweltering living room drinking our Cokes and talking, I couldn't help but notice how very pale Mrs. Phillips' skin looked. It was like she'd never been out in the sun. In fact, the whole time Junior and his mother lived there—which as it turned out was only a couple of months or so—I never saw her outside their apartment. Tanning wasn't the big rage then that it is today. Many women, including movie stars, avoided the sun in order to maintain the youthful appearance of their skin. Since Hedy Lamarr had pale skin, I guessed that Mrs. Phillips wanted pale skin, too.

Junior and I looked at each other's comics, while his mom paged through some movie magazines. All too soon, an hour had flown by and I could see by the clock on their wall that it was time to head home. I hated to leave the presence of Junior's mother. My eyes couldn't get enough of her, although I tried to be discreet about glancing at her so frequently. I told Junior I had to get going, thanked his mom for the Coke, and told her it was nice meeting her. She couldn't have guessed how much I really meant it. I gathered up my comics and walked over to the door.

As I paused just before leaving, Mrs. Phillips came over to me and extended her delicate hand. As she did, she was close enough that I could smell her perfume. It sure smelled good — like gardenias. I knew enough about manners to realize it was appropriate to shake hands as a gesture of friendship. Her hand was so soft and warm that it made me tingle just touching it. She looked right at me with her dreamy brown eyes and in her soft voice said, "I *really* appreciate you being Junior's friend. We've moved around a lot and that's made it hard for him to get to know other kids his age. So, thanks." And, with those words, she lightly grasped my upper arm, bent forward slightly, and kissed me on the cheek.

Wow! I felt like I'd been kissed by Hedy Lamarr. I was so flabbergasted I didn't know what to do. I'd never in my life been kissed by a woman other than my own mother or other female family members. And certainly never by a woman who looked like a movie star. I must say it was a sensation that I found quite enjoyable in a way that I hadn't experienced before. Looking back on it, this occurrence may well have signaled the beginning of my puberty.

I know I must have flushed from embarrassment, but I didn't care. I told Junior and Miss Lamarr—I mean Mrs. Phillips—goodbye as I floated out the door and down the sidewalk. When my feet again touched the ground at my house, I went inside and put my comics away. Mom was still in the kitchen and I let her know I was back. She asked, "How was your visit with the new boy?" Before I could answer, she looked at me more closely and quickly added, "What's that on your cheek?" Oh, no! It must have been the imprint from Mrs. Phillips' bright red lipstick. I, then, had a lot of explaining to do. I went over the whole experience in detail with Mom asking plenty of questions along the way. When I finished, she said bluntly, "I don't want you going back in that boy's house ever again. Do you understand me?"

"But, Mom, why not? Junior's a nice guy. And, his Mom was nice, too." Little did Mom know exactly how nice. I neglected on purpose to tell her about Mrs. Phillips' amazing similarity to Hedy Lamarr. To have done so would, undoubtedly, not have helped my case.

"You listen to me, young man. Those people are renters and transients. We don't know a thing about them. And, besides that, any woman who traipses around in a bathrobe in front of young boys in the middle of the afternoon is *not* the kind of woman you need to be around. Do you hear me? And kissing you? I can't believe she would do that. It's just not right. I've got a good mind to go down there and tell her so."

I pleaded with my mother not to go confront Mrs. Phillips about kissing me because her kiss had not been meant as anything other than an innocent expression of appreciation for befriending her son. I'd never seen my Mom so upset. I guess it was her overactive maternal instinct to protect her child from potential harm. In any case, I was absolutely forbidden to ever go back to Junior's again and that was that. Mom did make one small concession: Junior could come down to our house. As it turned out, however, that never happened.

My short friendship with Junior ended on the same day it began. I didn't want him to know that I couldn't come back to his house any more, so I avoided him completely. Whenever I saw him out on his step, I wouldn't even ride my bike past his house. This was really an awkward situation, and I felt bad about it. Later that summer, the Phillipses disappeared from their apartment in the big house on Wright Street as suddenly as they had first appeared.

I regretted the missed opportunity to develop a friendship with Junior beyond that one hour we spent together on a summer afternoon looking at comic books and drinking Cokes together. I don't know whatever happened to Junior and his "movie star" mother. I can only hope that he was able to overcome the concerns of any other overly protective parents and find a boy somewhere to become his *true* friend.

The "big house" where Junior and his mother rented an apartment is still standing at the northwest corner of Wright and Sanders Streets. It is the *only* original structure that escaped demolition along the four blocks of Wright between Buchanan and Sanders Streets.

15

Route 9E-9

When I turned twelve, I became old enough to have a paper route. At the time, there were three newspapers in Indianapolis: *The Star*, a seven-day morning paper; *The News*, a six-day afternoon paper reportedly favored by many Republicans; and *The Times*, another six-day afternoon paper, but this one was favored by Democrats. At that point in my young life I didn't know one political party from another and didn't really care. I was certain, however, that getting up well before dawn and carrying papers seven days a week was not for me. This narrowed my choice to one of the two afternoon papers. Actually, there was no choice. Since my Dad was a district circulation manager for *The Indianapolis News*, my decision was already made for me. I would carry the *News*; family loyalty demanded it.

The best part about my Dad working for the newspaper was that I got first crack at a choice route. *The News* divided the city into a number of distribution districts, each having a centrally located newspaper substation. The district serving the Fountain Square area where I lived was 9E, the one my Dad managed. As soon as route 9E-9 became available, I got it. This was an average-sized route of about fifty customers. A few lived in the seven-hundred block of Morris Street, some lived down the west side of the twelve-hundred block of Wright Street, and the rest lived on both sides of Sanders Street from Wright over to East Street. Since our house at 1218 Wright was ideally located about in the middle of this route, I already knew several of my customers as neighbors. Yes, 9E-9 was the perfect route for me.

Newspaper carriers were required to post a cash bond because they collected money directly from their customers and also were responsible for paying their weekly bill to the newspaper company. These bonds varied in cost with the size of the routes and the amounts of money handled by the carriers. The bond for my route was $20. Dad put up the money and allowed me to pay him back a dollar a week. I felt really good when I gave him the last dollar and paid off my very first loan.

In those days, *The News* cost just a nickel a day — only thirty cents a week for six-day delivery. This was an ideal amount to collect because some customers would give you two quarters or a half-dollar and tell you to keep the change. A twenty-cent tip was pretty generous back then and five of them quickly added up to an extra dollar. My route earned me about five dollars a week, plus tips. Not too bad for a twelve-year-old. It sure beat the fifty cents a week allowance I'd been receiving before becoming a newspaper carrier.

Collecting for the paper each week took much longer than delivering them. Every Friday after completing my route, I had to start collecting. Once in awhile a customer would stop me and pay me while I was delivering, but the official newspaper company policy was: deliver first, then collect. *My* rule was: take the money when you can get it—and I did. While collecting, if a customer wasn't home, guess what? I had to make another trip back later to try and catch them. Some people required multiple visits before I received my money. Every week it was the same routine.

In case you're wondering, yes, there were a few deadbeats in those days who would gyp a poor paperboy out of his money. In addition to not getting our meager profit, we were also required to pay for the papers that such people read and never paid us for. One of my biggest disappointments as a carrier was going to collect from a customer I hadn't been able to catch for a couple of weeks and finding their house — it was always a rental — empty. Such bums beat me out of sixty or even ninety cents. It amazed me that people had money for everything else, but couldn't come up with pocket change to pay for their newspaper. Thankfully, the great majority of my customers were honest people who always paid me on time.

Carriers were required to pay their paper bill by noon on Saturday — whether we'd collected it all by then or not. Since Dad was my district manager, I had an advantage: I never had to make the trip to the station to pay my bill. Dad always came home to eat lunch before taking his district's receipts uptown to the newspaper office. I, therefore, had the privilege of paying my bill at home. The other carriers were never any the wiser about this special arrangement that only I enjoyed. I kept mum and never bragged about it.

After having my paper route for a year or so, the newspaper company came up with a new way to increase their profits: they began offering magazines at discounted prices. For only fifteen cents a week, a *News* customer could choose up to three or four magazines from a long list of popular weekly and monthly publications.

The list included *Look, Life, Saturday Evening Post,* and many other favorites. We newspaper carriers didn't share in the extra profits generated by these magazine subscriptions. All we got were points for signing people up. The points were redeemable for a wide variety of mostly boy-oriented prizes like flashlights, pocket knives, and such.

The good thing was that the magazines were delivered in the mail and all we had to do was collect for them each week. The bad thing was collecting forty-five cents from those customers who took both the paper and the magazines. If they gave you fifty cents and said to keep the change, it was only a measly nickel tip. Under this new sales plan, it was obvious to me that *The Indianapolis News* was getting richer at the expense of our hard-earned tips. I voiced my feelings about getting skinned to my Dad. He was sympathetic, but all he could do was encourage me to go out and sell more magazines. Somehow, this seemed like it would only make the problem worse, not better. And, besides, I wasn't much of a salesman. Therefore, I never really got out and pushed the magazines like some carriers did. Can you blame me?

Since my salesmanship skills left much to be desired, I concentrated instead on providing excellent service. A missed delivery only counted against you if the customer called the newspaper office to report being missed. Such reports were called "complaints." In order to prevent having one of these, I gave all my customers my phone number and asked them to please call me directly if I ever missed them. I promised I'd get their paper to them quicker than waiting for the newspaper office to send one out.

I remember only one time ending my deliveries and having an extra paper. This was why it was so important to count your papers carefully when picking them up at the substation. I'd counted mine that day, as always, so knew for sure that the extra one meant I'd missed someone. Riding slowly back over my entire route, I came to a house I thought might be the one I'd missed. I took the paper up to the door and asked the customer if they'd gotten theirs. They hadn't and said they were just about ready to call me. My perfect record remained unblemished. I'm proud to say that, with the exception of this one "late delivery," I never truly missed a customer the entire time I had my paper route. My father shared my pride in this major achievement, although I'm sure he must have been disappointed in my poor performance at getting very few newspaper and magazine starts.

The newspaper company put great emphasis on reliable delivery to its customers. Those carriers giving perfect service for a year were invited to attend an annual awards ceremony. Trophies were given out with our name, route number, and the year engraved on them. Receiving one of those little "gold" statuettes of a newsboy on a pedestal made me feel like I'd won an Oscar. I earned three, one for each year I had my route. Along with the trophies came special newspaper bags bearing the title "Honor Carrier" (I never carried my papers in these because I used saddlebags on my route). There were also prize drawings, refreshments, entertainment, and local celebrities. The whole affair was quite a big deal, but Dad's pride in me was the best reward of all.

When I first got my route, carriers used route collection books with bound-in pages. Entries had to be written in to keep track of who owed and who had paid for each week. The books wore out easily, and carriers with large routes needed two books. At the beginning of 1953, the *News* introduced new and improved route books having preprinted cardstock pages, each with two holes prepunched at the top. The upper part of each page had lines for the customer's name and address. Below this were rows and columns of perforated stubs we called tickets. Each ticket bore the statement "PAID FOR THE NEWS WEEK OF" and the date. The tickets for "newspaper only" customers were printed in black; those for customers who also subscribed to magazines were printed in red. The color was a visible reminder whether to collect thirty or forty-five cents. When collecting, the carrier simply tore out the appropriate ticket and gave it to the customer. No writing was required. This clever system made it easy for the carriers to tell at a glance exactly who had and had not paid for a particular week, and it also provided the customers with receipts.

The pages were sandwiched together between a front and back cover made of thin aluminum; the whole set was held together by two metal snap rings. The book fit nicely in the back pocket of a pair of jeans. I filed off the corners of my book's covers so they wouldn't wear holes in my pocket. Some carriers occasionally hung their collection books from the handlebars of their bicycles. This, however, was a risky practice. I heard about a paperboy—no, it wasn't me—who'd lost one of his rings and hung his book by the remaining ring. Somehow, it came unsnapped as he was riding along and his collection book pages ended up scattered down the length of a city block. When you realized that those little tickets meant potential money in your pocket, it was not a good idea to take such a foolish chance.

The worst time of the year for a paper carrier was, of course, the winter. Cold temperatures and bad weather combined to make newspaper delivery a bone-chilling and often dangerous experience. Riding a bike on slick streets with fully loaded saddlebags was a real trick. On the other hand, the best time of the year for a carrier was Christmas. When collecting on the closest weekend before the big holiday, extra tips were usually given. Some customers would give you an extra half-dollar; others gave you a whole dollar. The most-treasured tip was the *silver* dollar. These seemed worth a lot more than a common dollar bill and once received were only spent as a last resort. They were something special to hold onto and brag about to the other carriers.

One of my customers gave me a wrapped Christmas gift each year instead of a cash tip. There was only one problem: the gift was always a box of Brach's chocolate-covered cherry cordials. Yuck! I loved chocolate, but hated cordials. They were way too sweet for me. In desperation, I'd bite off the tops, try to drain out the icky juice along with those disgusting preserved cherries, and eat just the chocolate shells. That still didn't eliminate all the syrupy filling. After giving up on making them edible, I'd give the rest of the box to my Dad. He thought chocolate-covered cherries were a real treat and told me he had since he was a boy. I was just glad to get rid of them. I'd much rather have gotten a cash tip, but I always smiled and thanked the lady when she gave me my box of cordials each year. She probably thought I loved them. Someone enjoyed them, but it sure wasn't me.

When I had a route, the newspapers weren't dropped off at each carrier's house. All the carriers had to report to their district substation to pick up their papers each day. I was a seventh-grader in elementary school when I first got my route. School let out at 3:15. After walking home in about fifteen or twenty minutes, I'd change clothes, jump on my bike, and head for the newspaper station. I never wore my school clothes while delivering papers. Why? Because when the papers came off the truck the ink was still fresh and would sometimes smear and get on your hands and clothing. The ink was difficult to wash off your skin and impossible to get out of your clothes.

Most newspaper carriers were boys my age or a year or two older. Station 9E had about thirty boy carriers and three or four girls. These brave gals had to endure a certain amount of "kidding around" and teasing at the station while waiting for the newspaper truck to arrive. We were all pretty innocent back then, so our banter was just in fun. Nothing that would be considered "sexual harassment" — most of us didn't know much about sex yet. The girls were tough enough to take a lot of guff from the boys. If things ever got a little out of hand, however, they'd run in and complain to my Dad. He'd call the offender(s) into his office, lay down the law, and that would be that — at least until next time.

The newspaper truck usually came in around four o'clock. In nice weather, the carriers would wait for it outside while talking about our bikes, our routes, who got the biggest tips, what was happening at school, or other such stuff. Some kids with yo-yos might show off the latest tricks they'd mastered. If it was cold or rainy, we'd all crowd inside. Our station was the back part of a one-story building which also housed the newspaper's regional classified advertising office. Nothing fancy, but it was warm and dry thanks to a big oil-burning heater. When we were all packed inside, the body heat alone from that many energetic kids could probably have heated the place.

When the truck arrived, it backed up near the station door. Some of the bigger boys would form a chain and pass the heavy bundles of papers from the truck into the building. They often took great delight in trying to make each other drop a bundle and look bad in front of all the younger kids standing around watching. Dropping a bundle never failed to produce howls of laughter and good-natured wisecracks.

As the boys brought the bundles inside, they stacked them on long wooden tables. These were sturdily built and had smooth Masonite tops so nothing would snag or tear the newspapers. Each bundle of papers had a protective wrapper of heavy paper around it and was secured with a tight band of strong wire. The station "captain" was responsible for cutting the wires and counting out the papers to each carrier. This time-consuming process might require standing in line for as long as half an hour waiting your turn.

Our papers occasionally arrived very late because of a press breakdown or a last-minute major news story had occurred that the newspaper company wanted to include in that day's edition. During such times, tempers sometimes flared and a couple of boys might get into a scuffle or a shoving match. Phil Eitel was the station captain; he was older, a high schooler. Phil would have to stop his distribution and break up the fracas. And he was big enough to do it. Nobody messed with Phil. Such conflicts were never too serious, but those involved were made to go to the end of the line, as well as have to suffer the inevitable gibes from their fellow carriers.

After receiving your papers, it was important to recount them yourself to be certain you'd received the right number. If you didn't, and discovered at the end of your route that you were a paper short, it meant making a long trip back to the station to get one. If, on the other hand, you completed your deliveries and had an extra, it might mean you had missed a customer. You wouldn't know for sure if you hadn't counted your papers (I always counted mine twice).

On most days, the newspaper company sent out a bundle of extras to each station and the carriers were encouraged to take a few and give them to *Times* customers in an attempt to convert them into *News* customers. There was a lot of competition between these two rival newspapers. The *Times* finally lost the battle and ceased publication several years later. Carriers at that time benefited by having numerous former *Times* subscribers along their routes who now had to start taking the *News* if they still wanted an afternoon paper. Boy, were they lucky. They got all those starts without even having to work for them.

Once you double-checked the count, your next task was to roll your papers. Remember, this was in the days long before newspapers started looking like giant tacos stuffed with ads, coupons, and other supplements. My Dad taught me how to fold the paper over twice, tuck it in, and twist the open end. This produced a tightly rolled paper that could be tossed up on a porch or stoop without having to get off your bike and carry it to the door. As I rolled my papers, I'd stuff them into the canvas saddlebags hanging over the luggage rack on the back of my bike. This produced a really wide load and required extra-careful maneuvering to avoid falling over. Sometimes, while still at the station, a kickstand would give way under such a load and some unlucky kid's bike would fall over on its side. Such misfortunes were yet another cause for laughter and taunts from fellow carriers. I know because it happened to me once or twice.

Back then, papers were not delivered by just tossing them on the driveway or throwing them in the yard as they are today. I prided myself in customer service—it tended to produce more tips. Some customers wanted their paper put behind their screen or storm door so it wouldn't blow away. Others, with exposed front doors, might request that I stick their paper behind the doorknob to keep it up off their stoop so it wouldn't get wet on rainy days. Whatever they asked for, I delivered. And it paid off, especially at Christmas.

I could pick up my papers at the substation around four or so, pedal back to my route, deliver them, and usually be home by five. When I think about it now, I realize that I made *less than a dollar an hour* for getting out in all kinds of weather and delivering papers six days a week. When you factored in the additional time spent in weekly collecting from my customers, the hourly pay rate was even lower. The extra tips may have helped as a motivator, but it still took a special kind of kid to be a paper carrier. And I'm proud to say that I was one of them.

Having a paper route was my first opportunity to earn money and get off the weekly allowances my Dad doled out to my two younger sisters and me. Learning how to be responsible, meet the public, sell a product, provide good service, make change, count money, pay bills, keep records, and maintain a savings account were all practical experiences that you couldn't learn anywhere else at any price at my age. Delivering *The Indianapolis News* on route 9E-9 provided all this, plus a lot of fun and good memories that have stayed with me through the years. And I can truthfully say that I had the *best* newspaper manager a carrier could ever have—my father.

The building that originally housed *The Indianapolis News* regional classified advertising office and circulation substation for District 9E is still standing on Virginia Avenue in Fountain Square, but has been extensively remodeled and repurposed. Additions to the back of the building (made in 2008) have completely eliminated the open area where the newspaper delivery trucks used to back in and unload.

16

The End of the Ice Age

Someday my grandchildren will probably think I'm so ancient that dinosaurs roamed the earth and people lived in caves while I was growing up. They will, of course, be way off the mark timewise. I did, however, witness the end of "The Ice Age." No, not the well-known period of history taught about in school, when glaciers covered much of northern Europe and North America. I'm talking about another time that came much, much later. It was an era when people still used iceboxes to keep their food cold.

I don't remember our family ever having an icebox. The last people on Wright Street who still used one of these antiquated appliances were the Taylors, an elderly couple who lived across the alley from us. I remember very little about Mr. and Mrs. Taylor except that they looked sort of like the "Ma and Pa Kettle" characters from a series of comedy movies popular in the early '50s. Unlike Pa Kettle, who always wore a derby hat, Mr. Taylor usually wore one of those flat caps like golfers used to wear. He liked to sit out on his front porch and whittle.

One day I sat and talked to him for an hour while he carved a little Indian in a canoe. When he was finished, he gave it to me. I was fascinated at how Mr. Taylor could turn a piece of wood into whatever he wanted it to be.

Mrs. Taylor wore her hair twisted up in a bun on top of her head and she always had on an apron. She also wore funny looking, saggy, tan cotton hose year round. Once in awhile, she'd come outside with a plateful of home-made gingerbread cookies still warm from the oven. She'd share them with any neighbor kids lucky enough to be playing out along the side-walk at the time. There are certain moments in life when you have to make your own luck. This was one of them. If the wind was right and my sisters and I smelled cookies baking next door, we'd make a beeline out to the front walk so we could be in position to benefit from Mrs. Taylor's kindness.

On certain days, we noticed that a red cardboard sign about eight inches square would appear in the front window of the Taylor's house. Large black numbers were printed on each corner of the card: 25, 50, 75, and 100. The card was positioned so that one of the numbered corners was on top. On the days the card was displayed, an odd-looking truck would drive up and park across the street from the old couple's house. The truck was painted all white. Two words in wide blue letters were on both doors of the truck's cab: POLAR ICE. The truck was driven by the iceman.

We never knew the iceman's name, but he was treated with a sense of awe by the neighborhood kids. The reason for this was partly because he was so big and brawny — very big, very brawny. This helped him perform his job of delivering ice. Whenever he pulled up in his truck and we were out in front playing, all activity ceased and we just stood there almost as if at attention. In silence, we watched him go through his unvarying delivery routine. He stepped out of the truck's cab onto the running board, climbed up over the low side of the open truck bed, and threw back a large flap of heavy canvas. It must have been white when it was new, but had long since turned a dirty gray. There, partly exposed, were stacks and stacks of foot-thick ice slabs.

The iceman pulled a pointed tool called an ice pick out of a holster on his belt and repeatedly stabbed in a straight line across one of the slabs until a large rectangular block broke free. The size of the block was determined by the number on the red card in the Taylor's window. He then slid the block of ice over to the tail end of the truck. Next, he jumped down to the pavement and threw a well-worn sheet of heavy black rubber over his right shoulder. Then, he grabbed the block of ice between the pointed ends of another special tool called ice tongs, stooped down, and pulled the block onto his shoulder. He did this in such a practiced way that he almost made it look easy. Finally, he carried that had-to-be-heavy block of ice up the Taylor's walk, climbed their front steps, crossed their porch, and entered their front door that Mr. Taylor would by now be holding open for him.

We didn't know exactly what the iceman did with the block of ice once he got it inside their house. I eventually found out one day when I was there to collect for the newspaper. Mrs. Taylor had invited me out to her kitchen to have a piece of fudge she had just made. While I enjoyed the chocolaty treat, she dug some change out of an old sugar bowl. As I waited, I noticed an unusual wooden cabinet and asked what it was. She said it was their icebox and that they used it to keep their food cold. Our family had a "modern" Frigidaire refrigerator, so I wasn't familiar with iceboxes or how they worked. Since the iceman made a delivery while I was there, I learned firsthand.

Mrs. Taylor opened a hinged lid on top of the icebox, reached down inside, and pulled out the small piece of remaining ice. She tossed it into the sink. The iceman then carefully lowered the dripping new ice block from his shoulder into the upper compartment of the icebox. The lower section of the box had two side-by-side doors. In here they kept luncheon meats, dairy products, and other foods that required chilling.

A galvanized metal pan about two inches deep sat on the floor below the icebox to catch water from the ice as it melted and dripped out through a drain hole in the bottom of the box. Mrs. Taylor told me they had to check the pan regularly and, when nearly full, her husband would empty it into the sink. I learned later that at the height of their popularity, iceboxes were available in several different sizes with various arrangements of compartments and doors. Most of the boxes were made of oak.

In those days, there were no ice cube trays or ice makers. If you wanted ice for a cold drink you had to chip pieces off the big block in your icebox. Since there was no freezer compartment in iceboxes, people bought all their meats fresh from the local grocer. It also wasn't possible to keep ice cream frozen at home. If you wanted ice cream, you made up a batch in a hand-cranked ice cream maker or bought some at the grocery and ate it soon after getting it home. Back then, groceries only sold ice cream in pints and quarts. There were none of the half-gallon or gallon-size cartons that are standard today. And for good reason. People couldn't eat that much at one sitting, so what would they have done with the leftover ice cream? They couldn't stick it in the freezer — *there was no freezer.*

On summer days, I can well remember seeing melted ice water trickling constantly over the tail end of the ice truck as it sat there at the curb during a delivery. As the truck went on down the street and swung around the corner onto Morris, water poured over the end of the truck bed like a miniature waterfall. You might think the ice company would have used en-closed, insulated trucks to protect the ice, but they didn't. While the iceman carried the heavy blocks of ice from his truck into the Taylor's house, he also left a trail of water drops. That's one reason why he used that piece of rubber sheeting over his shoulder, to keep his shirt from becoming soaked.

To my questioning eleven-year-old mind, it seemed that in the heat of summer the Taylors and other ice customers must be paying for more than they actually received. Maybe the iceman gave them a little extra to make up for the unavoidable loss from melting. I like to think that he did because he seemed like a nice man. He always waved with his free hand and said "Hi, kids" whenever he noticed us watching him carry ice into the Taylor's house. If we ran over to his truck and asked him politely, he would usually take a minute to chip us off some small ice chunks. There was no treat in the world like sucking on a free piece of ice on a sweltering Indiana summer afternoon. If he was behind schedule on his route, the iceman would say, "Sorry, kids. Not today. I'm runnin' late. Catch me next time." We'd all be disappointed, of course, but we understood. Experience told us that our patience would be rewarded in a few days the next time we saw him.

Eventually, old Mr. Taylor passed away; his wife moved to another part of the city to live with her son. We missed those times when she had brought out just-baked cookies and shared them with us out of her love for children. The house she and her late husband had lived in for so many years was put up for sale and now stood empty. The red sign disappeared forever from its front window. We never again saw our friend the iceman and his familiar white truck. There were no more free pieces of ice on hot summer days. The end of "The Ice Age" had come to Wright Street.

The Polar Ice & Fuel Co. facility that once stood on the west side of S. East Street just south of the Belt R.R. tracks was purchased and demolished for an expansion of the Stokely-Van Camp canning factory sometime in the late 1950s.

17

Dad Uses the F-Word

My dad was usually a gentle, happy man. Like many fathers, however, he had a temper that flared up from time to time. I could tell he was angry when he used any one of a select group of cuss words: the D-word, the H- word, and rarely — when he was really mad — even the nasty S-word. But I never heard him use the forbidden F-word. Not, that is, until a certain incident brought it forth for the one and only time in my hearing.

Dad's first brand-new car was a 1953 Nash Ambassador four-door sedan. This two-tone green baby was his pride and joy. The Nash was a large car that required ever-so-careful maneuvering in and out of our small single-car garage. We didn't have a lot of modern conveniences back in the '50s, but Dad did have an automatic garage door opener — *me*.

One of my duties as the only son was to go out to the garage before Dad did, unlatch the double wooden doors from the inside, swing them back out of the way, and secure them in their open position. A length of lightweight chain with a snap hook on the end was attached to each door. I'd snap the left door hook onto the wire fence that ran the length of our back-yard along the alley and ended at the garage. I'd snap the right door hook onto a big screw eye that Dad had embedded in a telephone pole at the intersection of the main alley beside our house and the cross alley behind us.

After he backed the Ambassador out of the garage, I'd unsnap the hooks, swing the doors back into their closed position, and lock them shut from the outside with an old bolt stuck in the hasp. If I was with Dad, when we arrived home in the car I'd go through the same process, only in reverse. This was all real handy for Dad and doing it made me feel trusted and important. My two sisters weren't expected to handle this responsibility; it was my job and mine alone.

One rainy evening Dad and I were com-ing home from some activity we had attended together. After he pulled up to the intersection of the two alleys, I reluctantly climbed out into the downpour and quickly performed my usual duty with the garage doors. This time, however, I made a serious mistake: I failed to snap the chain onto the fence to secure the left door. That door had a permanent sag that always made it drag against the grass. I (wrongly) assumed that this would hold the door in place long enough for Dad to pull in and didn't stop to think that the rain had made the grass slippery. I should have known better. Actually, I did know better, but was in too big a hurry. I was much more concerned about getting in out of the rain than I was in doing my job properly. After ducking into the garage, I confidently motioned at Dad to pull on in.

Dad saw my signal and proceeded to maneuver slowly forward. This was always tricky because of the offset approach required by the neighbor'sgarage which was directly across from ours and sat right at the corner of both alleys. Dad's garaging procedure was almost as complex and delicate as docking the Queen Mary. Just as the Nash's long nose entered into the safe harbor of the garage—BAM!—a sudden gust of wind blew the left garage door against the driver's side of the car. I guess Dad didn't want to move the car any further with the garage door rubbing against it, so he cranked down his window, reached out, and pushed the door away from the car. After it had swung back out of the way, he gunned the engine and the Nash lurched into the garage. I should have thrown myself under the car and avoided what was to follow.

Dad immediately jumped out of the car and slammed his door harder than usual. As he did, he uttered the unutterable word: "F_ _ _!" That vile word exploded out of his mouth with such force that it seemed to echo off the rafters and walls of our old wooden garage. This was my clear signal that, if I had any doubts about it, Dad was *really* mad this time. I didn't dare say a word. Since there were no lights in the garage, Dad told me to get the flashlight out of the glove compartment. I did, handed it to him, and he carefully examined every square inch of the car's left side.

Yes, he was mad and I knew exactly why. And he knew that I knew why. Nothing else needed to be said; it had all been expressed quite adequately in that one unspeakable word. At the tender age of twelve, I may not have fully understood the meaning of this taboo term, but I'd heard it used enough by older boys at school and by one of the barbers (an ex-sailor, I think) at the barber shop to have a pretty good idea.

Miraculously, the garage door impact had left no visible damage— *thank heaven!* If there had been a dent or a scratch on the car, I might've heard the word more than once, along with who knows what other dire consequences.

142

Dad calmed down immediately when he realized that all was well. He even apologized, "I'm sorry, son, but you know you're supposed to fasten both those doors back securely like I taught you."

I knew better than to offer any excuses — there was no excuse. All I could say in response was, "Yes, sir. It won't happen again."

He patted me on the back and said, "Good. And let's not say anything about this to your Mother. O.K.?" I agreed and the incident was over just that quickly. The rain slacked up a bit and I ran for the house.

That was the only time I ever heard Dad use the F-word. Believe it or not, the incident became a special bonding moment between us. His sudden outburst of anger and the resulting expletive remained one of those deep secrets shared only by a father and son. Luckily, the pristine ears of Mom and my sisters weren't around to hear what Dad said out in the garage that rainy night on Wright Street.

18

They Fell From the Sky

A terrific windstorm and heavy downpour swept across the southside of Indianapolis one midsummer evening. After the wind died down, my two sisters and I went out on our back porch to see if any damage had resulted. What a mess. The wind had blown scads of leaves, twigs, and branches out of our two trees and from others in adjacent yards. Our backyard was covered with tree litter. I stood there thinking about what a huge job I faced cleaning it all up, since yardwork was one of my responsibilities.

Rain was still pouring down and an occasional lightning flash lit up the low-hanging clouds. A large puddle had formed around the edge of the porch where the grass was thin. As we were talking about the storm, we heard a strange noise. The three of us went over to the corner of the porch, looked out into the yard, and focused our attention in the direction of the odd sound. It sounded like a cross between a kitten's mewing and some strange bird's cry. We'd never heard anything like it before. The sound was very weak; we couldn't tell exactly where it was coming from. By then, darkness was setting in and made it hard to see out into the rain. I hurried inside and got the flashlight. When I returned, the girls said the noise had continued now and then while I was gone.

I swept the light around in the yard while staying dry on the porch. Suddenly, I spotted something — actually *two* somethings — lying half-in and half-out of the far edge of the puddle. There in the flashlight's beam were two little squirming lumps of wet fur. One end of each hairy lump had a short, stringy tail; the other end had a tiny mouth squealing loudly. We didn't know what these creatures were, but they obviously needed help.

Sandy ran inside to tell our mother what we'd discovered. Mom came right away. She looked at the little squealers and told me to pick them up out of the puddle quickly before they drowned. She handed me the dish towel she had carried with her in her haste and said, "Here, put them in this." I jumped over the puddle into the downpour, scooped up the two bawling hairballs, wrapped them in the towel, and jumped back onto the porch as fast as I could. In just that short time, however, I was soaked.

The creatures were so tiny that, at first,

Mom thought they were baby mice. Or even worse, baby rats that may have been washed out of a sewer by the downpour. But they didn't have the pointy face typical of a rodent. They were kind of cute and looked like super-tiny kittens. As she wiped off the worst of the dirt and water from around their little faces, she decided that they must be baby squirrels. "Where'd they come from?" we wondered aloud. We'd never seen any squirrels living in our backyard. Our two trees had thin, spindly limbs, not the kind squirrels liked to build nests in. Both trees were healthy and had no hollow trunk that squirrels might live inside.

We were all totally mystified about where the squirrel babies had come from. Mom said maybe the strong wind had blown them out of a tree in someone else's yard nearby, or maybe even for some distance. In other words, they'd fallen from the sky. Wherever the babies came from, the storm had blown them into our yard and we felt obligated to take care of them.

Dad wasn't home that evening, so Mom took charge of the little critters. First, she carefully washed and rinsed each baby under the faucet in our kitchen sink to remove the dirt and bits of leaves that clung to their wet fur. They began shivering after she dried them off. Then, she had an idea: we'd use our kitchen's gas stove as a sort of drying chamber. We didn't have hair dryers back in those days. After lighting the oven, she lined a cake pan with a dish towel. After gently laying the squirrels in the pan, she stuck it in the oven.

My sisters and I thought this was funny, but risky. I asked Mom if it wasn't dangerous putting the squirrels in the oven—we were afraid she'd cook them. She said not to worry because she had only turned the oven temperature dial to its very lowest setting. She also left the oven door ajar so the heat wouldn't build up too much. Every few minutes she opened the door enough so we could all check and see that our two new babies were doing just fine.

After an hour or so, Mom pulled the pan of squirrels out of the oven. They'd thoroughly dried out by then; their coats were nice and fluffy, and they no longer looked like a couple of wet furballs. They were, however, mewing louder than ever. Mom figured they surely must be hungry. Since their eyes hadn't even opened yet, she knew with a mother's instinct that the babies had just been born and needed to nurse.

Mom thought of a perfect solution to the problem of feeding the hungry squirrels. She told my sisters to go get their baby doll nursing bottles. The bottles each had a small nipple that she thought would fit the squirrels' tiny mouths perfectly. The girls excitedly ran to get the bottles and were back in a minute. After heating up a pan of milk on the stove, Mom used a small funnel to carefully fill the two doll bottles. Then, she showed us how to nurse the babies from the bottles. Sandy and Jackie each fed one. I didn't have the mothering qualities of the girls, so I just watched in boyish fascination. The squirrels laid on their backs in my sister's hands and sucked on their bottles of warm milk. They soon drained the bottles and their little tummies were round and full. They quit mewing and were content at last. In no time they both fell asleep. Mom carefully laid them back in their pan and covered them with a washcloth. They looked so cute all curled up beside each other.

While they were sleeping, Mom said, "What are we going to call these little guys?" We all tried to think of some cute names that would be fitting for them. Several ideas were suggested, but none seemed to be the right ones. After thinking about it for several minutes, Mom finally came up with the winning names. She said, "Since we found them out in the rain and rain drops go pitter-patter, let's call them Pit and Pat." My sisters and I immediately agreed that these were perfect names. It didn't matter whether they grew up to be boy or girl squirrels, these names would fit them to a T.

So, Pit and Pat it was. I'm not sure how we determined which one was which; they had no distinctive markings. They must have been identical twins. Each of us kids thought we could tell them apart, although we often disagreed among ourselves about their identity. If the truth was known, we probably had them mixed up most of the time; but, it didn't really matter.

At first we kept Pit and Pat in an empty shoebox lined with a piece of an old bath towel. They outgrew the shoebox after several days and started moving around more after their eyes opened. The milk they eagerly drank every day must have agreed with them because they grew rapidly from week to week. Next, we kept them in an old bushel basket we found out in the shed. The squirrels soon grew even more active and wouldn't stay in the basket. Then, we kept them in a big toilet paper box I got from Fisher's Market. After awhile they could even clamber up out of the box without too much effort.

By now they'd developed tiny claws like needles which they could dig into the cardboard to make their escape. After getting out of the box, they'd scamper around the house, climb all over the furniture in the living room, and even go up the drapes. Sometimes, they'd hide from us until we coaxed them out with a few walnuts; they absolutely loved walnuts. Mom was having about enough of all this by now. She said, "Those squirrels belong outside, not running around in the house. Just look how they've starting to damage the furniture and curtains." Something had to be done and done right away.

A neighbor gave Dad an old rabbit cage to keep the squirrels in. Since the cage was too big to bring inside, we kept it out on the back porch. Right away it became obvious that Pit and Pat didn't like confinement. They began constantly chewing on the chicken wire that formed the top and sides of the cage. Their little pink mouths soon began to show signs of injury from all the wire chewing. We realized that, even though our squirrels were tame, they could not be kept in a cage.

Dad reluctantly opened the cage door one day and we all stayed in the house to see what Pit and Pat would do with their new-found freedom. They cautiously came out of the cage and explored around the back porch for a few minutes. Then, they climbed up one of the trees and jumped over onto the porch roof. During the next hour, as we watched, they built a nest using the towels and rags that had lined the floor of their cage. They tucked these up under the eaves of the house in a sheltered corner where the porch roof joined the back of the house. Dead leaves tended to collect there and the squirrels incorporated these into their nest.

Pit and Pat were free, yet they remained like pets. They still came when we called their names and ate nuts from our hand. Even though squirrels are wild animals, our two stayed so tame that they continued to let us pet them. They'd even sit on our shoulders. We kids didn't like letting them up that close to our faces, but Dad trained Pit to perch on one shoulder and Pat on the other — at the same time. He took great delight in getting them to do this trick. They'd do about anything for a walnut.

Pit and Pat stayed around for many months living in their nest under the eaves. Our interest in them began wearing off some as we saw less and less of them. As they became older they could fend for themselves without us feeding them. They eventually answered the call of the wild, moved out to find mates, and began living their lives without further close human contact. The nest they built was no longer occupied. Once in a while after that, however, we'd see a squirrel on the back porch and throw out some nuts — walnuts, of course. We never knew for certain if it was Pit or Pat, but there was no doubt in our minds that it was one or the other of them.

My sisters and I grew up considering ourselves lucky to have had the most unusual pets on Wright Street. We'll always remember them and how they literally fell from the sky and landed in our backyard on that stormy evening.

19

Totally Naked

Most twelve-year-old boys have never seen a totally naked woman — at least, they aren't supposed to. Maybe they've seen their mother diapering or bathing a baby sister and noticed there was a "difference" below the waist. Or, they may have snuck a peek at their father's or an older brother's girlie magazine. They may even have looked with curiosity at one of those nasty little cartoon booklets called "eight-page bibles" that teenage boys used to pass around on the sly. Yes, they might have seen photos or drawings of naked females; but how many had seen a living, breathing, fully mature woman bare from top to bottom? Not very many. I, however, was one of those few who did. Here's the way it happened.

My parents were good friends with our neighbors Woody and Marge Lyons. The Lyonses and their five kids lived just two doors up on our side of Wright Street. Their kids' ages overlapped those of my two sisters and me, so we played together frequently. The Lyonses were a fun family. We always enjoyed spending time with them. Mr. Lyons was tall and thin, wore horn-rimmed glasses, and had receding dark hair that was cut short. Mrs. Lyons was average height, had shoulder-length wavy brown hair, and was what they used to call pleasingly plump. This included having a much bigger-than-average bosom, maybe from nursing so many children.

Early one summer evening, the Lyonses were coming to our house for a backyard picnic. Getting together and eating outside wasn't always called a cookout in those days. My father had our charcoal grill all fired up and was ready to start grilling a mess of hot dogs and hamburgers. The Lyonses were running late and hadn't shown up yet. Dad wanted to know when to put the meat on, so he sent me to their house to find out how much longer they'd be.

I walked up the steps onto the Lyonses' porch and knocked on their screen door; their doorbell had never worked since we'd known them. While standing there, I noticed that the split in the bottom screen panel was longer than ever. Mr. Lyons sure wasn't much of a handyman. Donna, one of their daughters, came to the door. Seeing that it was me, she said to come on in. I wouldn't usually enter someone's house without being invited by an adult; but, since our families knew each other so well, I went on in. I asked Mary, the oldest Lyons girl, how soon they were coming down. She said it would be a few more minutes; her folks were still getting ready.

Suddenly, we heard a commotion upstairs. A child was giggling loudly and Mrs. Lyons was yelling "You better bring that back here, young man or you're gonna get it!" The sound was coming down their stairway which was out of sight on the other side of the far living room wall. Then we heardfeet thumping down the wooden steps. The bottom of the stairs ended at the edge of a large arched doorway that was right across the room from where I was standing.

In an instant, Tommy, the mischievous three-year old in the family, burst through the archway into the living room. He was dragging a white bath towel which he dropped when he spotted me. Tommy was closely pursued by his mother — who was absolutely, totally, 100 percent *naked*. She looked like one of those full-figured nudes from a Rubens painting. Instead of reclining on a velvet couch, however, she was chasing a naughty boy who ran off with her towel.

Mrs. Lyons immediately froze when she

saw me standing there. Did she do a quick about-face and run back up the stairs? No. She just stood there as if suspended in time and space. I couldn't help but see her — *she was facing me and only ten feet away.* We stood there gaping at each other, paralyzed in wide-eyed mutual disbelief like deer caught in the headlights of a car. I couldn't believe what I was seeing. In that incredible instant my eyes zoomed in on her and I could see every freckle and drop of water on her still-wet skin. I saw everything there was to see from her head down to her toes. And, believe me, I mean *everything.*

Finally, the magic moment ended. In reality it couldn't have lasted over a second or two. Then, in a panic, she grabbed up the towel Tommy had dropped and tried to wrap it around her derriere. But she wasn't fast enough. I'd already seen what she was trying to cover as she turned and bounded back up the stairway screaming all the way until I heard a door slam.

The slamming door snapped me out of my momentary trance. All the Lyons kids were practically rolling on the floor laughing about their mom's total exposure and my total embarrassment. I don't know who was more mortified, Mrs. Lyons or me. Probably me, since she'd fled the scene and left me standing there being laughed at. I told the kids I'd better go and we'd see them later at our house. They were still laughing so loudly as I left that I don't think they even heard me.

When I got back home, Dad asked me when the Lyonses were coming. I didn't know whether to say anything about what had just happened or not. I had my fingers crossed that maybe there would be no mention of it when they came. The way Mrs. Lyons had screamed up those stairs, however, made me think that our unplanned encounter was *not* going to be forgotten so quickly or so easily. I felt certain I was going to be in really big trouble because I'd been in the wrong place at the wrong time and seen "things" a twelve-year-old boy wasn't supposed to see. Like most kids would, I instantly decided to delay my inevitable punishment as long as possible by not telling on myself. So, I answered Dad truthfully, "They'll be down just as soon as Mrs. Lyons gets dressed."

Twenty minutes later, the Lyonses arrived. The kids trooped in first, still snickering about what had happened. They must have been given orders not to dare mention "the incident" because none of them did. I couldn't even look Mrs. Lyons in the face. My cheeks still felt hot from my humiliation. Mr. Lyons headed over to the grill and began talking to Dad. After a couple of minutes, they both started laughing, but Dad had a strange look on his face when they glanced over at me. I knew good and well what they were talking about. Since Mr. Lyons didn't seem upset about it, I hoped that his wife wasn't mad either.

After the picnic was over and the Lyonses had gone home, Dad asked me to help him clean the grill. My sisters were both inside helping Mom with the dishes. While Dad and I were alone, he said, "Well, son, Mr. Lyons told me about you getting quite an eyeful of his wife when I sent you up to their house earlier." He grinned in a knowing way. "But don't worry about it. He's not mad and neither is she. In fact, he told me that after she calmed down, she actually thought it was funny. They both realize you didn't do anything wrong and it wasn't your fault that you saw her the way you did."

I said, "That's good, 'cause I sure didn't mean to see what I saw."

"Did you really see," he paused and raised his eyebrows, "*everything*?"

I replied, "Yeah, Dad. *Everything.*"

He hesitated, then continued, "Then I guess you could see for yourself that a woman is made differently than a man. Have you got any, uh, questions about anything you saw?"

We hadn't yet had the traditional father-and-son talk about "the birds and the bees." So, at that point I still didn't know much about a woman's private parts. Boys my age knew that woman had various sizes of those lumpy things we called "boobies" (one of several names for them), but it was that "other thing" I was curious about. I hadn't yet gone through puberty, so my body was still as hairless as the day I was born. This left me with a burning question that I just had to ask. "Dad, why did Mrs. Lyons have *hair* down there?" I asked as I motioned toward my crotch. I wasn't even sure what to call the thing she had in place of what I had. We spent a really long time cleaning the grill while Dad did his best to answer my original question—and several others I thought of while we were talking.

Since it was getting dark, Mom yelled out the back door asking us why we were taking so long. Dad hollered back that we were nearly finished and we'd be right in. After our little man-to-man conversation that night, Dad never mentioned "the incident" again. Everyone else who knew about it seemed to forget it, too—almost like it had never happened. Life quickly returned to normal on Wright Street, but I had taken a giant step on my journey toward becoming a man.

20

The Man with No Nose

Most of the kids in our neighborhood — including my two sisters — were afraid of a certain man. We didn't know his name or where he lived. He'd occasionally come walking down our alley to get his car out of a garage he rented in a former livery stable building across the alley from our backyard. He was old and tall and lanky and often smoked a funny looking little corncob pipe. There was one other thing that made this man unlike anyone we'd ever seen: *he didn't have a nose.* In its place he wore a skin-colored cloth patch taped over the area where his nose should have been.

Three rumors about his missing nose were known along Wright Street. The first rumor said that he was a veteran who'd fought in World War I and his nose had been shot off by a German sniper. The second rumor was that he'd had a terrible disease called cancer and it had eaten his nose off. The third rumor said that he'd been in some kind of awful accident and his nose had been torn off or injured so severely that the doctors had to remove it. In those days before plastic surgery and the miraculous facial restorations that are so commonplace today, any of these rumors seemed believable.

When The Man With No Nose came down our alley and we were out playing in the backyard, he always spoke to us if he caught our attention. And, as you can imagine, he always did. We would usually just stand there gawking at him and maybe say a weak "Hi" in reply. We'd been taught by our parents that it wasn't polite to stare at people, especially people with something "wrong" with them. I'm afraid that's a lesson we didn't learn very well. We couldn't seem to help ourselves. His appearance was so unusual, what else could we do? My sisters would sometimes even run into the house if they spotted him approaching from a distance. I never joined their silly stampedes. After all, I was twelve, too old for such childish behavior.

One afternoon while I was out in the alley trimming weeds along our fence across from the old livery stable, the man must have come up the alley behind me while I was focused on my task. Suddenly, I heard a voice say, "Hello, young man." I turned and looked up from my squatting position; there he was, not three feet away. He introduced himself as Mr. Humphreys and asked me my name. I told him and we talked for a couple of minutes about the hot weather, what I was doing, and where he was going. I tried not to stare at his missing nose while we were talking, but it was hard not to.

When our conversation was about over, I committed a serious social blunder that went against everything I'd been taught. Most boys are born with a natural curiosity and I must have had a double dose of it because I dared to ask Mr. Humphreys what had happened to his nose. He looked down at the ground and was silent for a few moments and I instantly regretted having asked. Instead of getting mad, or telling me it was none of my business, however, he actually seemed pleased that someone cared enough to ask.

He said, "That's a good question, young man. Let me tell you about it." Mr. Humphreys told me that when he was thirteen, he got a boil on the side of his nose. His parents took him to their family doctor who lanced the boil and drained it. But his nose became badly infected and he developed blood poisoning which started spreading. The doctors at the hospital had to surgically remove his nose in order to save his life. I couldn't help but feel sorry for him when I heard this.

He went on to say that later they made

165

him an artificial nose from a new kind of plastic. But he didn't like the way it looked and was always afraid it wouldn't stay in place. He said, "I didn't want my nose falling off in my soup," and chuckled. I had to smile when he said this. As a result, he had quit wearing his plastic nose years ago. "It really isn't so bad not having a nose; I'm just glad to be alive," he said. So, as it turned out, none of those neighborhood rumors had been true. Mr. Humphries wasn't a war casualty after all. He also never had cancer and he hadn't been in a terrible accident.

After finishing his explanation, Mr. Humphreys looked at his pocket watch, wound it a few times, and said he had to hurry along to his doctor's appointment. He stuck out his hand and shook mine with a strong grip.

"It was good to meet you, Charles. Don't work too hard," he said with a grin. After adding a good-bye, he opened the doors on his garage in the old stable building and pulled out in his long black De Soto. Then, he closed the doors and climbed back in the car. As he started to drive away, he waved and smiled at me again. I waved and smiled back at him as the De Soto chugged slowly down the alley toward Wright Street.

After wiping the sweat off my forehead

with the back of my hand, I returned to my trimming. While chopping at the weeds, I thought about how unfortunate it was that Mr. Humphreys had lost his nose just because the new "wonder drug" called penicillin—which easily cured all sorts of infections—hadn't been available back when he was a boy not much older than me. How very sad.

From that day on, I was no longer disturbed by the appearance of The Man With No Nose and quit thinking of him in that childish and unkind way. Now, he was a real person with a real name. He was my new friend, Mr. Humphreys.

21

Tortured by Hillbillies

When I was a kid, the Nutgrass family lived on the other side of Wright Street and down one house from us. The Nutgrasses weren't natives of Indiana, they were Kentuckians. And to Hoosiers, all people from Kentucky were hillbillies. This was used more as a descriptive term and not so much in a derogatory way. They were just people who happened to have been born on the "wrong side" of the Ohio River. In those days, to us a hillbilly was generally someone born in Kentucky who had moved up to Indiana to get a "good job," loved Country and Western music, was a heavy smoker, cooked with lard, ate lots of homemade biscuits, and went "back home" every other weekend to see their kinfolk. This description fit the Nutgrass family perfectly.

Being a hillbilly when I was a kid didn't make a person a total social outcast, although it always carried a certain stigma even back then. Hillbillies were not so much looked down upon as looked askance at. They weren't yet universally thought of as being barefoot yokels who lived in shacks on the sides of mountains, inter-married with their cousins, made and drank lots of moonshine, and loved possum meat. All these colorful details became permanent additions to the hillbilly stereotype over the years thanks in large part to the once-popular "L'il Abner" comic strip and, later, to television shows like "The Beverly Hillbillies."

The radio over at the Nutgrasses was playing from morning till night. If you were on their side of the street, you could hear it in the summer when all their windows were wide open. Their next-door neighbors could probably hear it constantly since the houses were close together and weren't insulated in those days. Thankfully, their music was never so loud that we could hear it clear across the street. What I did hear when out on the sidewalk or while playing in our front yard, however, was more than enough to cause me to develop a genuine dislike for this type of twangy music accompanying whiny-voiced singers who all sounded pretty much alike to me. This dreadful stuff was officially called Country and Western on the record charts, but I grew up thinking of it as just plain old hillbilly music.

One of my buddies as a boy was the Nutgrasses' youngest son, Eugene. He was my age, so we were in the same grade at school. All of us kids called him Gene. The only person who called him by his full name was his mother. Whenever we were out playing together and she wanted him to come in for supper, she'd yell out their front door at the top of her voice, "EUUUGEEENE!" He'd just shake his head, roll his eyes, and run for the house. I liked Gene and never really thought of him as a hillbilly. Maybe he was adopted.

When we were talking one day, I asked Gene what his father did for a living. He told me that his dad worked as a "knocker" at Stark and Wetzel. This was one of two large meat-packing companies in Indianapolis that pro-vided hundreds of "good jobs" to hillbillies. I'd never heard of a knocker, so Gene asked his dad to tell me about it. Mr. Nutgrass explained that his job was standing all day astride a narrow chute down which cattle were driven one-by-one. As they came under his legs, he said he'd swing a heavy sledgehammer high over his head, and smack them right between the eyes. This knocked the cows out and was the origin of his unique job title. He went on to describe in gory detail how the unconscious beefs were then strung up by their hind legs, their throats were cut by another man with a special hook-bladed knife, and they bled to death. He said the men wore high rubber boots because they were wading around in blood up to their ankles. After hearing this gruesome story, I could hardly eat meat for several days—especially beef. It's a real wonder I didn't grow up to become a vegetarian. I eventually was able to get Mr. Nutgrasses' graphic job description out of my mind and returned to my old eating habits.

Mrs. Nutgrass wasn't a typical stay-at-home housewife. She had a full-time job along with her husband at S&W, although in another department I'm sure. Whenever I was over at Gene's and his mom was home, she always had her hair up in curlers and was usually smoking a cigarette. She stayed inside most of the time, so my Mom and the other neighbor ladies never developed friendships with her. I think she may have been shunned, not because she was a hillbilly, but because she was the only woman on our block who dared to smoke. Most women back then hadn't yet acquired this "evil habit." For some reason the Nutgrasses' house never smelled like cigarette smoke, but it did have a distinctive odor that I couldn't identify. It reminded me of the smell of hot chocolate, even though I never saw any of them drinking any.

Gene had an older brother who was in

high school. Everyone called him "E.T." Remember, this was decades before the famous science-fiction movie by that title, so his nickname didn't come from the film. When I asked Gene what his brother's initials stood for, he looked around to be sure E.T. wasn't in the house. Then, he swore me to secrecy and told me in a hushed voice that E.T. stood for "Elmer Tuggle." I could see why he went by his initials. Elmer was even worse than Eugene as a boy's name back then. I didn't ask where his one-of-a-kind middle name came from. E.T. was a head and a half taller than Gene and me. While not exactly fat, E.T. was headed in that direction. His puffy face and squinty eyes gave him a mean look and his mouth wore a permanent smirk. He had a bad reputation whispered around the neighborhood of being a bully. Gene was a good kid and my friend, but E.T. was something else. I was half afraid of him.

One day when Gene's parents were both at work, I was over at his house. E.T. and his ever-present buddy, Eddie something-or-other, came in. I never liked E.T., or his skinny sidekick, even though they'd never done anything to hurt me. Maybe I was spared because I was a buddy of his kid brother. Anyway, sitting around talking as boys will, we somehow got on the subject of the war and how the Germans and Japs had tortured their prisoners. One of their most infamous methods supposedly was stringing up captured soldiers by their thumbs to make them talk. Somehow or other, our discussion ended up in the Nutgrasses' garage out behind their house.

E.T. and Eddie were going to show Gene and I how this torture must have been performed. We were eager to see how and gullible enough to let them demonstrate on *us*. They tied long pieces of lightweight cord around each of my thumbs and ran the cords up, across two of the exposed rafters, and back down. Then, they made Gene and I stand on our tiptoes with our arms stretched straight up over our heads while they tied the other ends of the cords to Gene's thumbs. I wasn't wanting to continue by then, but went along with it out of fear of what E.T. might do to me if I didn't cooperate. I wasn't reassured by the fact that Gene seemed even more afraid that I was. He knew his brother — and what he was capable of doing — better than I did. If Gene was scared, I was plenty scared.

Everything was O.K. at first, as long as we stayed up on our toes and kept from pulling on the cords. After a few minutes, however, our toes started aching and one or the other of us dropped down a little to relieve them. This tightened the pull on our thumbs and started them hurting really bad. Then, to make matters worse, E.T. and Eddie left us hanging there like a couple of idiots and walked out laughing their heads off at our predicament. Our thumbs hurt so badly that Gene and I started crying and yelling out for help, but no one came to our rescue.

Finally, our two tormentors had mercy on us — probably because they were afraid a neighbor would hear us hollering — and came back to release us. We'd hung there only about ten minutes, but it seemed like hours. Our thumbs were sore for days, but we suffered no permanent injury. It's a good thing I was never a P.O.W.; I don't think I could've taken it. If tortured by this diabolical method, I probably would've betrayed my best friend or given my tormentors any information they wanted — anything to obtain release from the intense pain of being hung by my thumbs.

E.T. warned us not to tell anyone about this little incident in their garage or he and Eddie would beat the crap out of us. We must have believed him because Gene and I never told a soul. At least *I* didn't. I strongly doubted that E.T. would beat up his own brother, but I was pretty certain that with his and Eddie's reputations they might really beat *me* up.

After this traumatic experience, I quit going over to Gene's house when his parents were both gone and I knew E.T. was there. If I was over at Gene's and his brother came in, I made some excuse and headed home— pronto. Dad and Mom never seemed to notice this decrease in the frequency of my visits. At least, if they did, they never asked me why. And, even if they noticed, I don't think they really minded because they were never too happy about my spending time over there in the first place. Maybe it had something to do with the Nutgrasses being hillbillies.

22

New Jersey Joe's Front-Yard Fiasco

Across the street from our house was a double owned by the Sutherlands. Unlike most doubles, theirs wasn't built exactly the same on both sides. They lived in the smaller part of the house on the alley side and rented out the larger part to supplement Mr. Sutherland's income as a cab driver. Several families rented this side over the years. I don't remember any of them, except the Joneses.

The Joneses moved to Wright Street from somewhere in the northeast. New Jersey, I think it was. You could tell they weren't from Indianapolis because Mr. Jones always talked loud and fast. He also pronounced certain words a little differently than the way we Midwesterners did. He wanted everyone — even us kids — to call him "Joe." This was unusual in those days when children were still taught to address adults as "mister" or "missis". Dad and Mom said it was all right, so my sisters and I called Mr. Jones "Joe" like everyone else did.

Joe was a friendly, outgoing person. This made him perfect for his job as a territory salesman. He traveled all over central Indiana selling Flako corn bread and other boxed mixes. He carried cases of the stuff in his station wagon to give away as samples and to fill his smaller orders. Joe was the first person I ever knew who used business cards. He gave my folks one when our family went across the street to meet the Joneses. We were all impressed. Dad may have been a little envious because he threw the card away after we came home. I spotted the card in the wastebasket beside Dad's desk and retrieved it later when he wasn't around. The card went into my cigar box treasury for years although I'm not really sure why I kept it. I certainly didn't expect to be buying any Flako products. In fact, I didn't even like corn bread back then. I wondered at the time how a man could make a living just selling the stuff. I guess Joe was a pretty good salesman, a real wheeler-dealer who could sell about anything to anyone. Well, almost anything.

I don't remember much about Mrs. Jones except that she was petite. Of course, next to her husband, *everyone* seemed short. He was easily over six feet tall. Joe and his wife had only one child. She was about my age or maybe a year younger and had a peaches-and-cream complexion, curly blond hair, and the softest brown eyes I'd ever seen. Although I was just twelve plus several months, I was beginning to notice girls. And I sure noticed her. From the very moment we first met, I thought she was the prettiest girl there ever was. Even her name was pretty. All the other girls I knew had only one name, but she had two: Jo-Lynn. She was my first love, but neither she nor anyone else ever knew it at the time because it was my secret. Jo-Lynn was the *best* reason I remember the Joneses.

Then, there was the *other* reason. The corn bread business must have been a little slow that first winter the Joneses lived on Wright Street. Or, with Christmas coming in about a month, maybe Joe wanted to earn some extra money. Whatever his motivation, he came up with an idea never before tried on Wright Street. While looking out the window on a snowy, blowy Sunday afternoon, my sisters and I noticed that a flatbed truck was parked in front of the Joneses' house. We could hardly believe our eyes. Joe and the truck driver were unloading — of all things — *Christmas trees*. We called Dad and Mom to come see what was going on. They couldn't believe it either.

Back in those days, everyone bought "real" Christmas trees. They were the only kind available. The straight-as-a-stick aluminum foil trees were yet to come in a few years and the realistic, artificial trees of today were still far in the future. Joe no doubt thought he had a sure-fire money-making idea. Maybe he'd tried it successfully back in New Jersey. Fisher's Market was the only other source of Christmas trees in the neighborhood, so Joe didn't have much competition for his front-yard tree lot. He was probably seeing dollar signs as he arranged his sizable inventory of trees around the yard.

There was a problem, however; a very serious problem as it turned out. You might think that a Christmas tree was a Christmas tree. Right? Not so. People were very particular about their Christmas trees. And the people in our neighborhood favored trees that had short or medium-size needles, the kind that were prickly when touched. But Joe's trees had extra-long needles, the kind that were soft and droopy. Not only were the needles droopy, but so were the branches. We'd never seen such poor excuses for trees; where he got them we couldn't imagine. Joe had unfortunately committed one of a salesman's biggest blunders: he hadn't researched his potential customers' buying preferences. As a result, his big money-making plan was doomed to failure from the first day.

As if this wasn't bad enough, there was another problem with Joe's trees. They lacked the customary bases made from two pieces of wood in an X-shape and nailed into the cut end of their trunk. Later, Dad mentioned this when Joe was complaining about the slow — actually, no — sale of his trees. Joe said he wasn't going to bother with making any bases. He told Dad that most people just took them off and threw them away after getting their trees home, so why bother? He thought it was an unnecessary expense that would cut into his hoped-for profits. That may have been true, but most tree buyers expected their tree to have a wooden base. Some people who put up their tree for only a few days used the wooden base in lieu of buying one of the more up-to-date adjustable metal bases.

Since Joe's trees had no bases to stand on, he resorted to leaning them against his porch and around the trunk of a maple tree that stood in the center of his front yard. And, of course, every time the strong north wind blew down Wright Street, over went the trees. One would fall against another and they'd topple in groups like bowling pins. When he was home some evenings and on weekends, Joe spent most of his time setting trees back up instead of selling them.

Yet another problem was that Joe's trees must have been cut too early. Every time they fell over, out came needles — lots of needles. As a result, his trees began looking more and more scraggly. This sure didn't help their sales appeal, which was already close to zero. We'd see cars drive by and slow way down while the people inside them looked at Joe's trees. If he was out in the yard at the time, Joe would motion to them and encourage them to get out and look around. But they just shook their heads and drove away without buying a tree. They wouldn't even get out of their cars. Some of them looked like they were laughing as they drove off. That had to hurt. Joe, was a true salesman, however; he didn't give up.

Since darkness comes so early in December, Joe strung an electric extension cord out to the maple tree and hung a light bulb on it to illuminate his lot and facilitate evening sales. Unfortunately, this didn't produce the desired results. He began leaving the light burning all night. I guess he was afraid that someone might steal one of his trees. He needn't have bothered; no one thought they were even worth stealing.

Joe still worked at his regular sales job during the week. So, Mrs. Jones had to go out and stand up fallen trees all day while her husband traveled around his territory selling corn bread. He must have impressed upon her the extreme importance of minding the trees because she was out there every time the wind blew. Or so it seemed to us kids. My sisters and I frequently watched in amusement as Mrs. Jones repeatedly stood the trees back into their upright position. After all, you can't sell Christmas trees that are lying around on the ground.

After several days of doing this, we noticed that Mrs. Jones began just letting the trees lie where they fell. She started coming out only once a day — usually late in the afternoon when we were home from school to watch the show. We figured she wanted to make sure the trees were all upright before Mr. Jones came home from work. By then, the snow in their yard had become packed down and turned to ice from all the tramping around setting fallen trees back up. It's awful to admit, but the girls and I actually laughed out loud while watching little Mrs. Jones slipping and sliding around her yard wrestling with those trees — most of them were taller than she was. Kids can have a cruel sense of humor at times like these.

Joe ended up selling only *one* tree. My Dad bought it. He must have felt sorry for Joe, or maybe Joe gave him a good discount. In any case, Dad came home with one of Joe's dried-out, long-needled, droopy trees — even though we had always bought ones with medium-sized needles in the past. It was the sorriest-looking Christmas tree I remember us ever having. The branches were so flexible that it was nearly impossible to hang ornaments out on their ends. The decorations would just slide off and fall on the floor. As a result, a couple of Mom's favorite fancy glass balls were broken. She wasn't happy about it and let Dad know how she felt. This led to some heated words between them; it was one of the few times we ever heard our parents argue. Sometimes, trying to help out a friend comes at a high price.

We set the tree up in our red-and-green metal stand, the kind with a built-in watering pan. As the oldest child, I was made responsible for keeping the tree watered. After it sucked up a quart of water daily for several days, the rate of falling needles seemed to slow down a little, but never stopped completely. I know because it was also my job to keep the fallen needles picked up off the living room rug. I think if God had wanted to He could have created another whole tree out of all the needles that fell off ours.

As Christmas drew nearer and nearer, Joe

became increasingly desperate. He tried every-thing he could think of to sell his trees. He even lowered his prices, but that didn't help. People didn't care how cheap his trees were if they didn't want them in the first place. Finally, on the day before Christmas, after all hope was gone, Joe gave up. He hung out a hand-printed sign made from a cardboard flap torn off a Flako corn bread case. The sign read <u>FREE</u> TREES. I don't know if no one believed his sign or if ev-eryone who wanted a tree already had one by then; but, whatever the reason, he couldn't even *give* his trees away. On Christmas morning, my sisters and I looked out our front window at Joe's tree lot. It was just as full of trees as it had been when we last looked on Christmas Eve. Time had run out and Joe was stuck with all those unsold, untaken trees.

The leftover trees remained in the Joneses' front yard for weeks after Christmas. They looked for a time like snow-covered war casu-alties that had fallen on some wintry battlefield. After most of the snow had melted away, one by one the trees began disappearing. One day we spotted Joe dragging a tree in through their front door. We figured he must be burning them in their furnace. At least he saved a little coal and recovered part of his investment. Mrs. Jones probably wasn't too happy about having to clean up all the needles dropped by those trees being dragged through the house on their way to the basement, even though by then most of the needles had already fallen off outside. I could sympathize completely with how she must have felt. I'd bet she made Joe clean them up.

As a result of his failed effort in free enterprise, Joe went back to just doing what he did best: selling Flako corn bread. He must have learned a hard lesson from the experience because he didn't repeat his mistake the following year. And, sad to say, right after that next Christmas, Joe took another territory and the Joneses moved away. I never saw Jo-Lynn Jones, the pretty girl with the pretty name, again. Nor did I ever see another Christmas tree lot like her father's. But I'll always treasure my memories of her and of New Jersey Joe's front-yard fiasco whenever I remember Wright Street.

23

The Apple Core Incident

It happened on Saturday afternoon of the week before Christmas. Dad had picked up my sisters and me at our church after the annual childrens' Christmas party. As he drove along East Street headed for home, Dad decided to stop at Nilges' Bakery and pick up a dozen spice bars. These cookies were a great family favorite, especially with our father. He parked at the curb catty-corner from the bakery and left the engine running so we'd stay warm. While he was gone, Sandy, Jackie, and I were all sitting in the back seat discussing the good time we'd had and who we thought had played the role of Santa Claus. As we were talking, I munched on an apple that was in the goody bag I received at the party.

In those days, there was a silly little game kids played called The Apple Core Game. Whoever finished eating an apple would shout out, "Apple core!" Anyone within hearing distance could shout back, "Baltimore!" Then the person with the apple core would ask, "Who's your best friend?" Whoever had said Baltimore first picked someone. The apple eater would then throw the core at the designated person and try to hit them. Don't ask me what the point of this game was or where it came from. It was just something that we did back then for the fun of it.

One last bite of my apple and I was sitting there holding the core. I had to do *something* with it. So, almost without thinking, I shouted, "Ap-ple cor-r-re!" Both my sisters responded in unison, "Balti-mor-r-re!" (dragging out the "r" sound on the end of these two words was part of the game). I followed up with the required question, "Who's your best friend?" thinking Sandy would say Jackie, or vice versa. Instead, neither of them knew what to say since they both answered at exactly the same time. Just then, I looked out the window and saw a girl a little older than me walking past our car. To solve my sisters' dilemma, I quickly said, "How about her?" They both agreed, "Yeah, her." The official rules of the game then required that I throw my core at this unsuspecting victim whose back was now to me as she walked on by. I didn't really want to, but felt like I had no choice. Why did I have to go and open my big mouth?

I quickly rolled down the car window and

half-heartedly tossed my apple core in the girl's direction. I didn't try very hard to hit her; after all, I didn't even know her. The core just skittered harmlessly down the sidewalk past her feet. I knew she must have seen it, but I thought she'd walk on and that would be the end of the matter. Unfortunately for me, when I threw the core, the girl was approaching her house. How could I have known that she lived only one door down from where we were parked? She turned and ran up the steps. Just before going inside, she looked back at our car and gave me the dirtiest look I'd ever seen. Something made me think, "Uh-oh." I immediately started hoping that Dad would hurry back so we could make a quick getaway.

Hardly a minute after the girl went inside, she came back out on her front porch and pointed toward our car. Since ours was the only vehicle parked in the entire block, there could be no doubt that she was pointing at us. And, then, out of the door right behind her charged a bull of a man who was built like Bluto in the old Popeye cartoons (but without Bluto's moustache and beard). I tried to play innocent and pretended not to see him as he came down the steps and lumbered up to the side of the car. He rapped loudly on the window to get my attention and motioned for me to roll it down. This was obviously the girl's father, and he was fuming mad.

Bluto put both of his huge hands on the edge of the car's roof and practically stuck his head through the window. His face was red and veins were bulging out of his forehead. He was so close I could feel his breath on my face. It smelled like beer. "What's the idea of hitting my daughter with an apple?" he snarled angrily. I instantly reversed my thinking and fervently hoped that Dad would take his time and *not* come back while this guy was venting his anger. I didn't think Bluto would hit a boy who was only twelve, but he looked like he could easily start a fight with my father because of me. If Dad walked into this face-to-face confrontation, I'd end up in serious trouble—fight or no fight.

I was plenty scared; who wouldn't be? Along with my fear, however, I felt strongly that I was being unfairly accused of something I hadn't actually done. So, I dared to set the record straight about what had happened. The angry man panted heavily while awaiting my response. He spat out the words, "Well, what have you got to say about it?" After swallowing the egg-size lump in my throat, I meekly replied,

"Sir, it was only an apple *core* and I didn't really *hit* her with it, I just threw it in her direction playing The Apple Core Game with my sisters here."

He stood there silently blinking for a few seconds while my words registered in his mind. Maybe he was remembering The Apple Core Game from when he was a kid. Or maybe he'd never even heard of it, but didn't want to admit his ignorance by asking what I was talking about. In any case, he looked over at my wide-eyed sisters and said in a voice only slightly lower in volume, "Hey, you two. Is that what *really* happened?"

They both backed up what I had said by vigorously shaking their heads in the affirmative and replying nervously, "Y-Yes, sir." Their words seemed to cool him off. More likely, he was starting to notice the bitter cold and feel the brisk northerly wind blowing down East Street, since he had rushed out wearing only his trousers, an undershirt, and house slippers.

"Well, O.K. But watch out who you throw things at next time, *mister*," he growled as he stabbed his hot dog-size forefinger toward my face. Then he straightened up, turned around, and grabbed the girl by her upper arm. "C'mon," he said and escorted her toward their

191

house. It was all over as suddenly as it had begun.

As the man and his daughter hurried up
their front steps, the car window was still down.
I couldn't quite hear every word he was saying
to her, but it was something about not exagger-
ating things and getting him all worked up for
nothing. I sensed that he was now nearly as
upset with her as he had been with me a few
seconds earlier. I felt totally vindicated. Before
rolling up the window, I gulped some cold air
and started breathing again.

Dad came back to the car a few minutes
later smiling triumphantly and shaking a white
sack at us to indicate he'd obtained the much-
desired spice bars. After getting in the car, he
told us he'd been waiting for them to come out
of the oven and be cut to size. What perfect tim-
ing. He missed my entire encounter with Bluto
and was totally unaware of what had happened
while he was in the bakery. On the way home,
my sisters didn't say a word about the incident.
I think they were still in mild shock — I know I
was. They never told on me later, either. I owed
them each a free "no tell" for some future misdeed of theirs to repay them for keeping quiet
about this little dido of mine.

We took the still-warm cookies home and

wolfed them down with plenty of cold milk; Dad enjoyed his, as usual, with coffee. Those spice bars never tasted better. As a result of what happened to that scared twelve-year-old, you might think that he'd never want another apple in his life. But I still enjoy eating them. Whenever I finish one, I can't help thinking back to this unforgettable incident from my childhood. And, in my mind, I yell, "Ap-ple cor-r-re!"

The building at the southwest corner of S. East Street and Parkway Avenue that once housed Nilge's Bakery and apartments above it was razed several years ago.

24

A Lesson Learned

In spite of frequent report card notations about "talking in class," I took my public school education seriously, studied hard, and brought home good grades. My parents expected no less. While in school, I learned numerous interesting and helpful lessons from my books and teachers. I also learned other valuable lessons during my younger years the hard way: by experience.

One day my mother asked me to go on an important errand for her. She needed a prescription refilled at Pantzer's Pharmacy. Pantzer's was located at the corner of East Street and Lincoln Avenue. This was quite a distance from our house (maybe two miles), but I had my trusty bicycle to get me there. Mom cautioned me, as always, to be careful. She gave me the little white pillbox from the drugstore and a five-dollar bill. I stuck them in my pocket and off I went.

On my way down East Street, I rode past Weddle's Drugstore. Suddenly, I had what I thought at the time was a great idea: why pedal all the way down to Pantzer's when here was a drugstore closer to home? I was probably about thirteen at the time and should have known why this idea wasn't workable. I innocently, but ignorantly, believed that you could just go into any drugstore and get prescriptions refilled as easily as you could go in and buy over-the-counter items. How wrong I was—as I soon found out.

No one was visible on the sidewalks in all four directions as I parked my bike on the wide concrete area in front of Weddle's. So, I didn't even bother locking it. I went up the two steps and through the weather-beaten wooden entry door into the store. The window in the door was covered with so many decals advertising Alka-Seltzer, Doan's Pills, Ex-Lax, and various other drug products that you could hardly see through it. As the door opened and closed it rang one of those old-fashioned jingly bells on a spring to announce my arrival. Once inside, I glanced around and quickly spotted the pharmacy section a short distance from the door. As I walked up, the lady behind the counter smiled and asked, "May I help you?"

"Yes, ma'am. I need to get this prescription refilled," I replied as I handed her the pillbox. She took it from me, glanced at it, and raised her eyebrows. Then, she carried the box over to the pharmacist who was working busily a few steps away.

"Bill, this young man wants to get a prescription refilled," she said with a slight smirk. The pharmacist looked at the box, pointed at something on the label, rolled his eyes, and shook his head negatively. The lady nodded in agreement. She returned to the counter where I stood wondering what was going on. "I'm sorry young man, but we can't refill this prescription," she said as she handed me back the box. Genuinely puzzled, I immediately asked, "But why not? The label says right here that it can be refilled one more time."

The lady looked at me over the top of her tortoise-shell glasses as if she didn't know exactly what to say. She turned toward the pharmacist and said, "Bill?" The pharmacist stepped out of his work area where he must have overheard our conversation. He cleared his throat and said, "Son, the reason is that this prescription was originally filled over at *Pantzer's* Pharmacy." He emphasized the name as he said it. "See? Their name's right there on the label." He pointed toward the pillbox I was holding.

I looked down at the box label. Right at the top in white script letters on a blue background the label clearly said Pantzer's. But I already knew that. I looked up and replied politely, "Yes, sir. I know."

"Well, this is *Weddle's*." This time, he over-emphasized the name as he said it. Still not understanding what he was getting at, I asked, "You mean you can't just refill it here and save me a trip to Pantzer's?"

He chuckled and then answered with far more patience that my youthful ignorance deserved, "I'm afraid not, son. I wish we could, but the only people who can legally refill a prescription are the ones who have the original doctor's order on file." He was probably wondering how anyone could be so stupid. I stood there in awkward silence while my mind processed this new and unexpected information.

Finally, it dawned on me just how dumb my request had been. As I stuck the pillbox back in my pocket, I apologetically responded, "I'm sorry; I didn't know." I could feel my cheeks reddening from humiliation as I stood there wishing I was invisible so I could run out the door without being seen. The next few seconds were like a scene from a nightmare. I had to plod what seemed like a mile to that door with feet that felt like they weighed a hundred pounds each. And all in slow-motion. While making my exit, I heard the clerk and the pharmacist laughing about something. It wasn't too difficult to figure out what that something was. Their laughter sounded like it was being amplified over loudspeakers as I closed the door behind me.

Once outside, I hurriedly jumped on my bike and pedaled on down East Street to Pantzer's. It was only another three blocks further. They refilled the prescription without any problem and I biked back a different way so I wouldn't have to go past Weddle's. After arriving home and putting my bike away, I took the medicine in and gave it to Mom along with her change. She thanked me for going after the pills, but I never told her what I'd gone through to get them. As I turned to walk away, she noticed my cheeks and asked me out of motherly concern why they were so red. I replied that it must be because it was really hot out and I'd ridden in the sun most of the way — which was true. But, of course, that wasn't the *real* reason for my red face.

Yes, I'd suffered extreme embarrassment, but I found out firsthand how pharmacies and prescriptions work. I also learned a valuable lesson that has served me well through the years: don't be too quick to take what seem like easy shortcuts in life. By the way, I never set foot in Weddle's Drugstore again.

The building at the northwest corner of S. East Street and Terrace Avenue that once housed Weddle's Drugstore was razed many years ago after it was gutted by a fire. Pantzer's Pharmacy was located in a large brick building with a distinctive gabled tile roof at the southeast corner of S. East and Lincoln Streets. The building now houses a laundromat.

25

Into the Wild Blue Yonder

Several boys in my neighborhood shared a love of anything to do with airplanes. One summer, some of us—including Ivan Charley, Gene Nutgrass, Steve Staples, and myself— started an Aero Club. Our main purpose was to build and fly model airplanes. Ivan, who had far more experience in doing this, would share his knowledge with the rest of us, who were all just beginners. Since we had limited incomes at our age, we couldn't afford the expensive models powered by miniature engines that ran on special fuel and were radio-controlled. Instead, we had to be satisfied with the far less-glamorous, but much more affordable, rubber band-powered models.

Our first group project was for everyone to buy a certain airplane kit sold at the Ace Leather & Hobby Shop. Then we'd meet together and build them. After they were all completed, we planned to have a "fly off" to see whose plane performed the best. These weren't realistic scale models of airplanes like in the kits common today. These were stick-and-tissue-paper planes built to fly, but not to look like any actual airplane.

The kit included everything needed: sticks of balsa wood, yellow tissue paper, a tube of Testor's model glue, lightweight tires, a red plastic propeller, a long heavy-duty rubber band for powering the prop, and miscellaneous pieces of hardware. We all bought our kits and met together at Ivan's house over on Sanders Street. He showed us beginners how to hold our wings and tail pieces in place with straight pins on a sheet of waxed paper, so that when we applied the glue it wouldn't leave a mess on anything. We assembled our kit planes, glued all the frame pieces together, and basic construction was finished except for adding the tissue paper to the wings and tail surfaces. Some of us had to go deliver our paper routes, so the meeting broke up before we had time to complete this step. We all agreed to finish our planes at home and get together the next day to give them their flight tests.

I proudly carried my airplane framework up the block to my house, hoping I'd see someone I knew along the way, so I could show it off. It was a foot long and had a wingspan of about fourteen inches. Quite impressive — at least, I thought so. But, you might know, I didn't pass a single person along the way. After getting it home, I put my plane on the workbench in my room and left to carry my papers.

Hurrying back after finishing my route, I still had about an hour before supper. I really wanted to see how my plane was going to look when finished, so I went ahead and applied the tissue paper to the wings and tail surfaces. While we ate supper, the glue on the paper had time to dry. After we finished eating, I hurried up to my room and began putting the finishing touches on my very first hand-built, flyable airplane. On a sudden impulse, I decided to name it the "A-1."

After trimming away the excess tissue paper and attaching the wheels, propeller assembly, and rubber band, the A-1 was finished. What a beauty! As I admired the plane sitting there so proudly on my workbench, it looked ready to take to the sky. I couldn't wait until tomorrow; I had to give it a try right then. The others in my family were all out on the front porch. I'm not sure why I didn't round them up to watch the maiden flight of my airplane. Maybe I was afraid it wouldn't fly and I'd be embarrassed. In any case, I took the A-1 downstairs and out into the backyard without the crowd of cheering onlookers that it deserved.

A flat, smooth concrete walk about a foot wide ran down the middle of our yard. The walk made a perfect runway from which to launch my balsawood beauty.

I carefully held the nose end of the thick wooden stick that was the main body frame piece using my left thumb and my index and middle fingers. With my right index finger, I carefully began winding the propeller round and round. As I did, the rubber band attached to the back of the prop hub began twisting. This twisted band stretched back to near the tail end of the plane and provided the stored energy that powered the plane — the more turns of the band, the more revolutions of the prop and the further the plane would fly. Ivan had warned us not to overwind the rubber band; doing so could cause the main body to snap under the strain. I wound mine until the wooden frame was starting to warp a little. Seeing that, I decided I'd wound it a few too many times and backed off several winds until the body looked straight again. Only then did I notice something that in my excitement I'd completely missed: I'd wound the prop in the wrong direction. Boy, was I glad no one was there to watch because my plane wouldn't have flown at all. If anything, it would likely have shot *backwards*. Upset by my stupidity, I held the plane tightly, let the prop spinout completely, then rewound it correctly in the opposite direction.

At last, the A-1 was ready for takeoff. Twilight time was fading fast. The sun had just dropped below the horizon, but there was still enough light. Not the slightest breeze was stirring; it was dead calm — perfect for the launching of a super lightweight model plane like mine. I sat it down at the very end of the walk with its tail right next to the back porch so there'd be as much runway as possible for the takeoff. Our garage loomed just thirty feet away at the other end of the walk. If the A-1 didn't take off quickly and gain altitude rapidly, it would smash into the garage. I guess I was optimistic that such a tragic fate could never befall my plane.

Holding my breath in anticipation, I let go of the prop and it started spinning powerfully. Then, I let go of the tail and the plane started its takeoff roll. Slowly at first, then with increasing speed, it taxied straight down the walk, bobbling slightly each time it ran over one of the expansion joints in the concrete. About halfway down the walk, its wheels lifted clear and the A-1 became airborne. Hur-raaay! It was flying; it was actually flying.

My next concern immediately became whether or not the plane would clear the garage. At first, it looked like there was no way for it to climb that high in such a short distance. Almost miraculously, however, the A-1 rapidly gained altitude and cleared the peak of the roof by several inches. I stood there proudly watching my creation silently soar into the twilight sky toward the last rays of the sunset. It was like a scene from a movie.

After the plane flew over the garage roof, it kept going and started losing altitude as the rubber band wound down. After a few seconds it disappeared from sight behind the roof. I finally snapped out of my adolescent state of awe and realized that my plane was headed for parts unknown. I quickly opened our side gate and ran down the alley in the direction my plane was headed when I last saw it. The backyards of the houses over on Sanders Street ran parallel to our garage. The A-1 had been flying straight as an arrow when last seen, so I knew it had to be in one of those yards.

Several minutes went by; it was starting to get dark. I frantically looked for my lost plane, but couldn't find it anywhere. Some of the yards behind our garage had dense grape arbors in them and others had small trees, but the A-1 wasn't visible in any of these, at least not from the alley. I even ran upstairs to my bedroom window and anxiously scanned the neighbors' yards with my three-power binoculars. But by then it was getting darker and I really couldn't see very well. I finally had to give up my search.

I didn't say anything to my family about losing my brand-new airplane; I was too ashamed to admit what I'd done. I went to bed that night terribly disappointed to say the least. As I lay there, unable to sleep, I kept thinking over and over how I should have launched the A-1 from an open, clear area where I could have easily retrieved it and flown it again and again. Hours of fun could have been mine, but it was not to be. I thought what a waste of the time, money, and effort I'd spent building that airplane — and all for nothing. Now I wouldn't be able to participate in the club competition. Who knows? The way the A-1 performed on its one-and-only flight, I just might have won. Unfortunately, I would never know. And all because I couldn't wait until tomorrow.

The next morning, I had one last desperate hope. I asked all the people on Sanders Street into whose yards my plane might have landed — or, more likely, crashed — if they had found it. None of them had. Most of them knew me because they were customers on my paper route. They were all sympathetic and even let me go into their backyards to look for the plane myself. No luck. It was almost like the A-1 had flown into a time warp or entered another dimension and was never seen again.

What happened to my plane after its one magnificent flight into the wild blue yonder that unforgettable evening out in my backyard on Wright Street? I wondered then and I still wonder now. I'll *always* wonder.

The entire street floor of the building that once housed the Ace Leather & Hobby Shop (and Wade's Drug Store) is now the Fountain Square Branch of the Indianapolis-Marion County Public Library. The two stories of offices and apartments above have been converted into senior citizen housing.

26

Rocket Fuel Reaction

Dick Foster was my best buddy all during our grade school, junior high, and high school years. I spent way more time over at his house than he ever did at mine. The main reason for this was that I had no brothers, but Dick had an older one, Clyde, and a younger one, John. So, something was always going on at the Foster's. They enjoyed a lot more "freedom" than we did at my house and had a lot more fun as a result.

One day I rode my bike over to Dick's to see what he was up to. He lived just a few blocks away on Woodlawn Avenue over near Fountain Square. When I got there, I found Dick, John, and a couple of other boys from their neighborhood out back in the Foster's ramshackle old garage. They were busily engaged in something that would excite any normal, red-blooded, American boy: they were making and setting off rockets.

Rocketry was a subject of great interest during the late 1940s and the decades following. The fascination started near the end of

World War II. Germany had fired thousands of their infamous V-2 rockets against England and other Allied targets in Europe. These missiles caused widespread terror, damage, and death, but they came too late in the war to affect its inevitable outcome. As the war ended, the U.S. Army captured and shipped home a large number of unfired V-2 rockets, along with many of the Nazi scientists who had developed them. Our armed forces recognized the great potential of rocket-powered missiles in future warfare and began developing and testing many types and sizes. As a result, the newspapers and popular magazines of the day were filled with rocket photos, news articles, and features. Naturally, boys our age ate it up.

The Fosters and their friends had read an article in *Boys' Life* magazine detailing how to make and launch small, solid-fuel rockets. The key word here was *small*; these miniature rockets were only about an inch-and-a-half long. They were nothing to compare with the sleek foot-long or even yard-long kit rockets sold in hobby stores today. The boys were making their rocket bodies by hand from aluminum foil, or "tin foil" as we called it. The bodies were easily made by rolling a foil strip several times around a match stick or a large nail. The tube was then removed and one end was pinched into a crude point. These were definitely "one-shot only" rockets because the burning fuel always left holes and gunky residue in them.

When I arrived, some of the boys were ever-so-carefully peeling the foil liners off the outside of chewing gum wrappers to obtain the precious material needed for rocket bodies. That explained why they were all chewing such huge wads of gum that they could hardly talk. Since Mrs. Foster didn't have any aluminum foil in her kitchen, there was no other source readily available. So, some Einstein among them had come up with the idea of using gum wrapper foil. It must have seemed like a good idea at the time, but it had obvious limitations. I guess it was a good excuse to chew lots and lots of gum.

Dick's job was preparing the solid rocket fuel. This was done simply by shaving the heads off wooden kitchen matches using a single-edge razor blade. After shaving several matches, he used the blade to chop the larger pieces into smaller grains. Then, he'd fill one of the foil rocket bodies with the granulated match heads. Launchers were improvised from a small-diameter piece of metal tubing or a strip of metal or wood with a groove in it. The launcher was set up at a shallow angle to the ground to support the rocket during ignition and to give some direction to its flight path.

To ready the rocket for firing, it was placed in or on the launcher with its open end pointing toward the ground. Ignition was achieved by holding a lighted match against the rocket's tail. The fuel inside would catch fire, burn in a flash, and the exhausted gases pushing out the open end gave the rocket its forward thrust. These tiny rockets worked on the same basic principles as their many-times larger counterparts under development by the U.S. military.

The range of the tinfoil rockets depended entirely on how finely the solid fuel was chopped and how densely it was packed into the rocket's body. They'd fly anywhere from a yard to several yards. Occasionally, one of the rockets when ignited would just sit on the launcher and burn up without going anywhere. But even these incidents were a cause for excitement.

I was fascinated by what was going on and wanted to be part of it. The boys immediately accepted me as a member of the Woodlawn Avenue Rocket Club. I was truly bitten by the rocketeering bug. Dick showed me what to do and how to do it. I jumped right in and soon felt like a young Werner von Braun, the famous German rocket scientist. Over the next couple of hours, we began experimenting with how to improve our rockets. Since everyone was getting sore jaws from chewing so much gum, one of the boys came up with an alternative idea and ran home. He returned a few minutes later grinning from ear-to-ear as he proudly displayed a long sheet of foil he had begged from his mother. This kitchen foil was thicker and stronger than the kind used on gum wrappers. With this new supply of superior material, we started making our rockets a little bigger. But this required more fuel and more match head shaving to produce it.

The larger rocket bodies could still be made quickly and easily in less than a minute. What took so much time was the shaving and chopping up of the match heads needed to fuel the rockets. Working together, we made and launched rockets as fast as we could produce enough fuel for them. After an afternoon of rocket building and launching, it was time for me to head home. I promised Dick I'd help out by shaving some match heads at my house and bring the fuel back with me the next day. I was really excited. The more fuel I could make, the more rockets we could launch tomorrow.

As soon as I got home, I checked our supply of kitchen matches. We had only one box and it was half empty — not nearly enough. I went to my room, checked my hidden cash stash, and took out what I thought was more than enough money for several boxes of matches. Then, I asked my Mother if I could run over to Fisher's Market to buy something for a "science project" I was working on — which was basically true since rocketry is a science. She said O.K., but it was with hesitation in her voice. I hurried to the store before she changed her mind and soon returned with three large boxes of Ohio Blue-Tip Matches. Now I had the raw material needed to go into full-scale rocket fuel production.

Since it would be an hour or so until Dad came home and we'd have supper, I decided to get started right away. My upstairs bedroom was a typical attic room with two long sections of sloping ceiling. Along one wall, Dad had built me a wooden workbench which I used for all sorts of projects. It was the perfect place to make solid rocket fuel. In my junk box, I found a metal canister lid about four inches in diameter; it would work as a collecting pan. I dug a couple of razor blades out of my tool box and was all set. I eagerly began cutting and scraping the heads off the first box of matches. An hour later,

I'd finished that box and started on the second one.

The next thing I knew, my father was home and coming up the stairs to my room. I didn't panic because I honestly felt I wasn't doing anything wrong. I even thought Dad would be supportive of my project and be proud of me for my new-found interest in science. Mom must have told him about me buying the three boxes of matches. Naturally, he was curious—as any father would be—about what I was planning to do with them.

I was still shaving match heads when Dad reached the top of the stairs and walked around to where I was sitting at the bench. He could clearly see what I was doing, but must not have understood why I was doing it. In any case, he asked me, "What are you doing with all those matches, son?"

I proudly announced, "I'm shaving off the heads to make solid fuel for some little rockets that Dick Foster and I are making over at his house."

Dad didn't say anything for several seconds. I wasn't sure if he didn't fully understand what I'd just told him, or if something was wrong. His attention was totally focused on the sizeable mound of shaved match heads that I'd collected in the metal lid.

Dad finally spoke and said very forcefully, "I want you to stop *right now* and scoot back from the workbench." I did so without questioning why, although I was puzzled by the sudden change in his tone of voice. Dad then carefully picked up the lid of match heads and began carrying it toward the stairway. As he did, he said, "Bring all the rest of those matches that you haven't shaved yet and follow me." Now, I was totally mystified. What was going on?

I followed Dad as he slowly descended the stairs, walked down the hall, through the kitchen and rumpus room, and out the back door. As we crossed the back porch, he said, "Wait here." Then, he carried the lid and its contents to the center of our backyard and set it down in the middle of the concrete walk running out to our garage.

He backed up, turned around, and asked me for the matches I'd brought down with me. I handed him the box. "Now stand back—way back," he said with a wave of his arm for emphasis. I backed up to the porch, never taking my eyes off the precious supply of rocket fuel that I'd worked so hard to produce and was obviously about to lose. Dad looked me right in the eye and said, "Charles, let me show you what would've happened if you'd accidently struck a spark into these match heads upstairs at your workbench." He bent down and struck one of the matches on the side of the box, then turned and tossed the flaming match toward the metal lid.

The match hit its target and landed on the pile of match heads. In a split second — WHOOSH! — the pile disappeared into a column of fire that erupted from the lid and shot at least six feet into the air. And, then, it was gone just as suddenly as it had appeared. I could hardly believe it. In fact, I wouldn't have believed it if I hadn't seen it with my own eyes. I walked out to where Dad was standing and we both looked down at the metal lid. It was now completely empty and had a scorched spot in its center.

Dad said, "Now can you understand why I was so concerned about what you were doing upstairs?" His question evoked my immediate answer,

"Yes, sir. If those match heads had gone off upstairs that flame would have shot up onto the ceiling over my workbench."

"That's right," said Dad. "You could've set the house on fire. And, even if the ceiling hadn't ignited, you might have burned your face and eyes badly and maybe ended up scarred or blind for life. Hadn't thought about that, had you?" he asked.

All I could do was half hang my head as I shook it back and forth and said, "No, sir, I sure didn't. I'm sorry. I won't do that again." I was trying to show my contrition and that I had learned a valuable lesson, hoping to avoid punishment for my foolhardiness.

Since I hadn't realized the potential seriousness of what I was doing and no actual harm had resulted, my father decided that no punishment was required; he let me off with just his words of warning. The lid was already cool to the touch, so Dad told me to go throw it in the trash can. I did, but probably should have asked if I could keep it to show my fellow rocketeers. Not wanting to push my luck, however, I said nothing.

As we headed into the house for supper, Dad said with a grin, "That sure was quite a flame wasn't it?" I think the "little boy" part of Dad — the part that a father never outgrows — got just as much of a thrill out of seeing such a spectacular sight as I had.

"Boy, it sure was," I responded enthusiastically, but not quite daring to smile about it. "I still can't believe that just a bunch of match heads could create so much fire."

He squeezed my shoulder and said, "Son, just be more careful next time you do something unusual like that and try to think about the potential dangers. If you're ever not sure about *anything*, wait until you can ask me about it before doing it. O.K.?"

"Sure, Dad." I responded. That sounded like a pretty sensible rule to me. I've tried to follow it for the rest of my life, except that Dad is no longer here to consult with and to advise me. How often I've wished he was.

The next day, I could hardly wait to go tell Dick and the rest of the rocket club members about what had happened. After I told them, I was sorry I did. The guys wouldn't believe my wild story at first; they thought I was just pulling their leg. That burnt can lid sure would have come in handy as proof. Finally, after much retelling and invoking the cross-my-heart-and-hope-to-die oath of truth, I was able to overcome their skepticism and convince them that, like the Israelites in the Bible, I'd really seen a pillar of fire.

Right away, Dick's kid brother, John, wanted to try and produce our own, even bigger, fiery column. Unfortunately — or maybe it was fortunately — we were nearly out of matches and none of us had the money needed to go buy that many more. As a result, John's idea never got off the ground. It's probably a good thing that it didn't or this story might have had a different ending.

The novelty of making and launching rockets wore off quickly; we were already tired of the work involved in making the fuel required. So, one of the boys suggested we go play some Flies and Grounders. Everyone threw in with the idea. We rounded up the Foster's cracked and taped old Louisville Slugger, their beat-up ball with half the stitches missing, and two or three well-worn gloves. Then, we headed for the empty field across the alley for some good old baseball. It was always fun and was sure a whole lot safer than rocketry. But it couldn't compare with the never-to-be-forgotten thrill of creating a six-foot pillar of fire right in your own backyard.

27

Fisher's "Super" Market

Down at the corner of Wright and Sanders, half a block from our house, stood the biggest and best grocery on Wright Street: Fisher's Market. Six days a week, Fisher's opened at 8:00 am and closed at 6:00 pm, except on Fridays when they stayed open until 9:00. Fisher's was closed on Sundays, like all stores back in those days when the restrictive "Blue Laws" prohibiting Sunday sales were still in force. Seven-day-a-week shopping didn't come along until a few years later when it was introduced by the big national chain stores. But, even then, Fisher's remained closed on Sundays. And their loyal customers didn't mind.

Bill Fisher and his wife, Jenny, owned and operated the store. He was the manager and she served as the store's bookkeeper. Mr. Fisher was a lanky six-foot plus, had a prominent nose, and was mostly bald with a band of kinky gray hair around the sides and back of his very pink head. He spoke in an unusual, hesitating manner. Mrs. Fisher was average size and had short black hair. She was usually working up in the store office, so the customers didn't see too much of her. The Fishers had two children: an older daughter, Elizabeth, and a younger son, Carl. He worked in the store occasionally while a teenager.

The assistant manager at Fisher's was Billy Ressler. He was slender and almost as tall as the boss, sort of quiet, and had noticeable acne scars on his cheeks. His wife, Dorothy, worked in the store as a cashier. She was a little shorter than her husband, and had curly brown hair and a pug nose. Her pleasant personality made her a favorite with everyone. Dresses with bobby socks and loafers were Mrs. Ressler's regular outfit at the store. In cold weather, she sometimes wore slacks or jeans, but always with a dress over them.

My first real job was working as a stock boy at Fisher's for the huge pay of 75 cents an hour. Prior to this I had a paper route earning only a few dollars weekly. Working at the market enabled me to make about ten dollars a week. Not too bad for a high school freshman in those days. I was elated when Mr. Fisher hired me and I could quit my paper route. No more lugging heavy bags of newspapers around in all kinds of weather for me — I'd hit the big time.

Fisher's Market had been just another corner grocery when my family first moved to Wright Street. The store was originally housed in an old wooden, two-story building—dingy, overcrowded, and a firetrap. The downstairs of the house next door was connected to the store and used as stockrooms. About a year or so after I started working at Fisher's, it underwent a major remodeling and expansion.

The new Fisher's building was of masonry construction with large windows and modern fluorescent lighting to provide a bright interior. The store was air-conditioned at a time when most businesses and homes (including my own) still were not. How lucky I was to work at Fisher's on hot days. Mr. Fisher had the new signs on the outside of his store painted to read "Fisher's SUPER Market." He was justifiably proud of his new and improved store. It had become the largest and most attractive of all the five groceries along Wright Street.

Fisher's Market had no written job descriptions. My work as a stock boy consisted of doing whatever Mr. Fisher told me to do. Stocking involved bringing cases of food and other merchandise from the stockroom, cutting the cases open, stamping prices on the containers, and placing them on the shelves. Sacking groceries at busy times like Friday nights and

Saturdays was another big part of the job. Sweeping all the aisles at the end of the day and wet-mopping the entire store the last thing on Saturdays were regular duties. Taking out empty boxes and other waste and throwing it in the trash bin (there weren't any dumpsters in those days) occurred as needed. Once in awhile, I had to help pass out flyers door to door in the neighborhood to advertise special sale items. I never enjoyed doing this; it was too much like being a paperboy again.

All Fisher's employees were required to wear long, white, bib-top aprons while at work. The boss and his wife wore them, too. I never liked wearing an apron; I guess it made me feel menial. In our apron pocket, we stock boys carried two essential items: a razor blade for opening boxes and a small piece of steel wool for rubbing off old prices stamped on the ends of canned goods. On stocking days, we'd use a "potato masher"-type metal price stamper. These stampers had a built-in ink pad that required occasional re-inking. I found out once the hard way that you definitely shouldn't over-ink the pad. I did and ruined a good shirt as a result because the permanent purple ink I got on it wouldn't come out in the wash.

Once every couple of weeks, the Allied

Grocers wholesaler would deliver heavy cases of canned goods and big cartons of paper products and cereal. As you might imagine, we stock boys hated to see the trucks arrive. When these orders were delivered (if they were large ones), Mr. Fisher often called in the other stock boy to help the one already scheduled to work that day. The new merchandise had to sit in the aisles until we moved it into the stockroom or placed it on the shelves. Mr. Fisher didn't like the aisles cluttered because this made it difficult for his customers to maneuver through them. So, he was always on us to put away the new stock as quickly as possible. Sometimes, when he wasn't too busy, he'd pitch in and help us.

Fisher's Market was way ahead of its competition on Wright Street in many ways. Fisher's had not one, but two checkout counters. Each had a modern electric cash register, not the old-fashioned hand-cranked kind still used in most smaller stores. Pushcarts were provided for use while shopping, although they were much smaller than the huge ones used in supermarkets today. Fisher's offered free delivery in a panel truck while its competitors were still making their deliveries on bicycles. Customers could even call in their orders to Fisher's and their groceries would be selected and brought right to their door and carried inside to their kitchen. That was real, personal service.

Fisher's also offered buying on credit. The smaller grocery stores around the neighborhood couldn't afford to do this because they needed a constant cash flow to keep their doors open. Many customers coming through Fisher's checkout lines would routinely say "Put it on my bill" after their purchases were totaled up. When payday came, usually on Fridays, they'd stop by that evening when the store was open late, or on Saturday, and pay part of their balance. I wondered if some of them ever paid off their bill entirely. There were a few chiselers who moved away without paying off their grocery tab at Fisher's, but most people back then were honest and could be trusted. My parents believed in and practiced the "cash and carry" rule; they never resorted to using credit for buying our groceries. I sensed that my mother for some reason thought it was a social disgrace to do so.

Fisher's main cashier was Mrs. Elizabeth Murphy. Most everyone called her "Murph," but I wasn't allowed to use this nickname. My parents taught me respect for adults and expected me — with rare exceptions — to call them only by their last name. Mrs. Murphy was in her late fifties, had gray hair, was shorter than average, and wore silver-framed glasses. She didn't have much of a chin; it was more like a turkey wattle. She was friendly to everyone and was well-liked by Fisher's staff and customers. If you ever wanted to know about anything that was going on in the neighborhood, all you had to do was ask Mrs. Murphy. She heard all, knew all, and told all. Whenever I saw her speaking with someone in a low voice that no one could overhear, I knew she was sharing some neighborhood gossip too "juicy" for my young ears.

"Big John" Gutzwiller drove Fisher's delivery truck. He was gone a lot making deliveries or picking up special items needed at the store. He'd been a football player at Manual High School and looked like one, too: tall with broad shoulders, powerful arms, and a ruddy complexion. Big John was quiet, but had a good sense of humor and a warm smile. He was always friendly to us peons. Everyone working at the store, as well as the customers, liked John. After he graduated from high school, we really missed him when he quit Fisher's and joined the Navy.

Fisher's Market was famous in the neighborhood for its fresh meats. The meat department was run by a butcher named Charlie. He was middle-aged, slightly overweight, and had thinning black hair which he kept well oiled and combed straight back. Charlie was sort of a Casanova-type who liked to flirt with the ladies. Some of them enjoyed his flirtations, but others didn't. He seemed to know which were which and treated them accordingly. Charlie got by with it because Mr. Fisher must have thought it was good for business.

The other employee behind the meat counter was Doris. She sliced and prepackaged lunchmeat, sliced-to-order per customer requests, and filled other deli and meat orders from what was on display in the meat case. Doris was an average looker, short with curly black hair and blue eyes that had a certain sparkle in them. For some reason, her top button was undone most of the time so that the upper part of her cleavage was plainly visible, especially when she bent way forward to get a roll of lunchmeat up in the front of the meat display case. I was old enough by then to notice such things. Despite her captivating ways, Doris had a habit that I found really annoying: she was always giggling.

The other stock boy at Fisher's was Ronnie Morris, a friend of mine from our grade school days back at P. S. #13. Each Saturday, Ronnie and I were assigned by Mr. Fisher to work one of two shifts the following week. One shift was Monday, Wednesday, Friday, and half a day on Saturday; the other was Tuesday, Thursday, and all day Saturday. Mr. Fisher alternated us between the two shifts so that our hours averaged out the same each month. We usually worked two to three hours on weekdays after school. Working later on Friday nights had one drawback. If a Manual High School ballgame was scheduled that night, you had to miss it. Since Ronnie was a much bigger sports fan than I was, I would — with Mr. Fisher's prior approval, of course — work in Ronnie's place on an occasional Friday so he could attend a game. I was more interested in earning a little extra moola.

Working at Fisher's had certain "fringe benefits." One was occasional free eats. When I came to work late in the afternoon, if there were any leftover donuts from Sap's Bakery in the cardboard tray under the clear plastic cover, Mrs. Murphy would say, "Charles, you might as well eat those donuts. Nobody's going to buy them this late in the day." She didn't have to suggest it twice. I'd scarf them down immediately, even when they were a little dry or the glazing had turned "sweaty." Once in a while, there'd be unsold brownies left in the box; these

were an extra-special treat since I loved chocolate. Mrs. Murphy would say, "You might as
well eat those brownies, Charles, they're probably stale by now." I'd chomp them down, stale
or not. The donut and brownie tray always sat
on the end of the checkout counter, so I guess
Mrs. Murphy felt like she had control of them. I
think she really just wanted to get the box off
the checkout counter because it was in her way.
Mr. Fisher, if he noticed, never said anything
about not eating these leftovers since they
would have gone into the trash anyway. I always felt it was O.K. to eat them because an
adult had given me permission to do so—bless
that Mrs. Murphy.

Filling the old-fashioned Coke machine
with six-ounce glass bottles presented special
opportunities to enjoy a free drink. Whenever
Ronnie or I had the machine unlocked and open,
we usually helped ourselves to a free bottle. No
one ever told us that we could, we just sort of
assumed it was O.K. One Saturday, Mr. Fisher
saw Ronnie chugging a Coke and made a comment about remembering that they *weren't* free.
Ronnie dutifully dropped his nickel in the coin
box and no more was said about it. I was nearby
at the checkout counter and saw and overheard
the incident. From then on, I never drank any

more Cokes "on the house." I didn't want to risk losing my job over a nickel.

One day, I was restocking jars of whole dill pickles. As I pulled one of the big jars from the carton, I noticed something strange. In among the pickles, the jar contained several broken pieces of what looked like metal rod about the diameter of a pencil. I could have just set the jar on the shelf and gone on about my business, but I did what I thought was the right thing: I took the jar to show Mr. Fisher. He was up in the "conning tower," as we called it. The store office was built at a level several feet above the store floor, so he could keep an eye on things. This was one of the few times I was ever up there, since it was normally off limits to employees. He seemed quite impressed by my discovery and appreciated me bringing the jar to his attention. As I left the office, I felt like I'd saved the good reputation of Fisher's Market from being tarnished by selling contaminated merchandise. Shortly after that, I was given a ten-cent an hour raise. It paid to do the right thing.

In those days, when checking out at the grocery, there was no question of "paper or plastic?" — there was nothing available back then but heavy brown paper bags. Fisher's were imprinted with the AG logo and the store's name.

After carefully packing the bags, we'd carry them outside to the customer's car for them. If they lived just a few houses from the store, we'd even carry their bags home for them, if they requested it. Sometimes, there'd be a small tip for this extra service, but not always. Such services were expected and were part of the reason why people shopped at neighborhood grocers like Fisher's.

Some customers brought their own fabric or net shopping bags to carry their groceries home. Others who lived farther away or had more to carry would bring their own collapsible wire carts. They'd leave them just inside the front door of the store and we bag boys would load them when their owners checked out. Getting these heavily loaded carts down the two steps from Fisher's floor level to the sidewalk wasn't always easy. If a customer was older or frail or looked like they might need help for some other reason, we'd roll their cart down the steps for them. Again, personal service was our specialty.

Outside, near the store's front door, stood two large wooden chests on short legs with hinged, locking lids. The Wonder Bread Company and Colonial Bread provided these delivery drop-off boxes. Their route men stopped at

Fisher's so early in the morning that the store wasn't open yet. They'd leave freshly baked bread and buns—probably still warm—in the boxes. Then, when the store opened, someone had to carry all those baked goods inside and stock the bread shelves. I never performed this special duty because I didn't work mornings. I wondered if Fisher's received a discount since they had to do their own stocking.

Sitting on the breadboxes was a favorite hangout for the neighborhood kids while they drank a Coke or ate candy and other treats they bought at Fisher's. If none of them had bought anything at his store and they were just goofing off, Mr. Fisher would go out and tell them not to sit on the boxes or hang around. But they often got by with it because he was too busy to notice them. If they didn't make too much noise, Mrs. Murphy would usually tolerate it and not rat on them to the boss.

One day, Mrs. Murphy noticed a bunch of rowdy boys on and around the breadboxes. Mr. Fisher was away from the store on business, but she knew what his rules were. So, guess what? She sent *me* out to run them off. Enforcing rules with your own peers isn't easy. Luckily, these were all good kids; I knew most of them. They didn't like my eviction notice too well, but gave me no trouble and soon went on their way. Mrs. Murphy dutifully reported her observation and my enforcement of store rules to Mr. Fisher when he returned. I scored a few points with the boss because of it, but I would just as soon not have been placed in the role of an enforcer. It just wasn't me.

After working at Fisher's Market for over two years, I moved on to a better-paying, part-time position as a draftsman. I'll always be grateful to Mr. Fisher for giving me my first chance at a real job. It may not have paid much by today's standards, but at the time it was good money for a boy my age. The opportunity it provided for me to interact with and learn about other people was a valuable experience in my maturing process as I grew up on Wright Street. You can't put a price on that.

Fisher's Market was razed in the mid-1960s for construction of the huge southeast interchange of Interstate highways 65 and 70. Harry's Meat Market (a smaller store at the southeast corner of Wright and Prospect Streets) was also torn down as part of this project. Owen's Market (a much smaller grocery at the southwest corner of Wright and Morris Streets) had gone out of business and been converted into apartments a few years prior to this. Two smaller groceries south of Fisher's held on for awhile, but within a year or two closed their doors forever and were converted into housing which is still occupied today. One of these stores (name unknown) stood at the northwest corner of Wright Street and Parkway Avenue. The other was Payne's Market (at the northeast corner of Wright Street and Cottage Avenue). Payne's had been previously operated under a different name for several years by another owner.

28

Breaking a Record

The 1940s were known as the Big Band Era. The mid-1950s were a time of transition from these large orchestras and mellow singers of the past to the beginning of something new and wildly different in the musical world. I was a teenager during this historic shift. I never cared much for the Big Band sound, but had begun developing a taste for many other musical types. I couldn't read music or play any instrument, but I sure enjoyed *listening* to music.

When my parents bought a new, smaller "modern" radio, I inherited our family's old one: a Detrola multiband. This was a big table-model radio with a wood cabinet, an illuminated tuning dial, and a four-inch speaker. An eight-foot antenna wire ran out the back. I stretched this aerial across my room and, by patiently twiddling three dials, I could pick up everything from police calls to foreign language broadcasts to ham operators. My radio transported me to places far beyond my house on Wright Street. But, best of all, my radio picked up stations from all over the United States. And many of them were playing a brand-new kind of music called "rock-and-roll." I loved it from the first time I heard it and listened every minute I was up in my room—even many nights after I was supposedly in bed asleep. The first rock song I remember hearing was Bill Haley and His Comets belting out "Shake, Rattle, and Roll." When I heard it, something stirred inside me; I absolutely *had* to have that song.

Late on a winter afternoon, I braved the cold and walked down Morris Street to the Fountain Square Record Shop on Shelby. A strong wind was blowing the entire time making the six-block trip seem much farther. Upon entering the store, I found it so warm inside that I felt like I'd stepped into an oven. Whew! Boy, was it hot.

I was the only customer in the place. Looking around, I saw bin after bin of records sitting on sturdy wooden tables. The cracked walls were randomly plastered over with posters and publicity photos of recording artists. Dirty white paint was flaking off the old tin ceiling; chips lay here and there among the records. A couple of bare electric light bulbs glared down from the ends of drop cords. This place was definitely nothing fancy, but I didn't care. All I wanted to do was buy a record.

The man who ran the shop asked me if he could help me find something. This was my first time in a record store and I didn't know my way around, so I told him I wanted that new song by Bill Haley. The man said I was in luck; they had one copy left. He quickly found the record, pulled it from its protective paper sleeve, plopped it on the turntable built into the front counter, and started playing it. This, I found out later, was customary to ensure that the record had been pressed properly and that it had no scratches. Keep in mind that back in those days songs were recorded on 78-rpm discs about ten inches in diameter. These recordings had only one song on each side: a hit song on the so-called A side and some lesser-known tune by the same artist on the B side.

Hearing the song over a big twelve-inch, wall-mounted speaker and at a volume much louder than I ever dared play my radio at home only made me want that recording more than ever. Satisfied that the record was O.K., the man slipped the black disc back into its sleeve and, then, slid it into a flat paper sack. I paid my 99 cents plus tax, thanked him, and headed for home. As I stepped out into the frigid air, it seemed to have grown even colder while I was in the store. Maybe it was just the sudden contrast with the shop's suffocating interior. As cold as it was outside, I preferred it to the heat inside. At least I did for the first few minutes.

As I hurried along, my hands started getting really cold, even though I was wearing a pair of knit wool gloves. I was afraid I'd drop my precious record if I tried to hold it in my cold, gloved hand. So, I stuck my hands in my coat pockets to try and keep them warm and held the record clamped securely — and I thought safely — under my right arm. Since this was the first phonograph record I'd ever purchased, I had no idea that in those early pre-vinyl days the material from which my record was made would become extremely brittle when cold. As I walked home through the twilight, the wind let up some and a few snowflakes began swirling down. I could feel them hitting my face, but I hardly noticed. I was thinking only of that exciting song I'd soon enjoy hearing on our family's record player. The words and tune spun through my mind as I hurried along.

After returning home, I laid the record down carefully and quickly took off my gloves, navy peacoat, and sock hat. Then, I opened the sack and slid out my record. I was ready to rock-and-roll. But, even before removing the record from its sleeve, something didn't feel right. The sleeve felt limp for some reason. Imagine my disappointment when I slowly pulled the record out and discovered that it was broken in two — yes, broken *in two*. All that held the halves together were the round paper labels on each side. Carrying that cold, brittle disc under my arm hadn't protected it at all. Instead, this was the very thing that had caused the record to break during my walk home. I just stood there for a few moments struggling with the fact that the record I had just purchased was actually broken. It seemed like a bad dream come true.

I never got to play my new record — not even once. How could I? It was in two pieces. Trying to glue it back together crossed my mind, but with a crack running clear across it, the record wouldn't have played very well and might have damaged our phonograph needle. I was absolutely crushed by this catastrophe. Here I'd frozen my fanny walking to the record store and back, spent my hard-earned dollar, and then — like a moron — had broken my record on the way home. I couldn't blame anyone but myself. The man at the store, who should've known about such things, could've warned me to be extra careful with the record out in the cold. But he didn't, and I wasn't. As a result, Bill

241

Haley and His Comets would *not* be rocking and rolling at the White house tonight.

Since the man had told me this was the last copy he had in stock, it wouldn't have done any good to run back and try to buy a replacement. Instead, I called the store to see when more copies of Bill Haley's big hit would be available. The man said he was expecting some any day; "any day," however, turned into several. Every two or three days I phoned to check and see if the shipment had come in yet. The guy probably got tired of my continual calls, but he kept encouraging me to not give up. I suppose he wanted to sell me another record as badly as I wanted to buy one.

While waiting on the record to come in, I still heard it on the radio from time to time, which only increased my desire for it. Finally, after a couple of weeks, the store received what I'd been so anxiously awaiting. I almost ran to the record shop and bought my treasured tune — for the second time. Taking no chances, I brought the record home by firmly, but carefully, grasping it with *both* hands. And I wore my fur-lined leather gloves to keep my hands warmer and give me a better grip. I carried that long-desired disc almost with the veneration of a priest handling a holy object.

This time, my replacement record made it home safely in one piece. I gently placed it on our phonograph out in the rumpus room and played it over and over. My two sisters heard the song playing and seemed to like it the first few times. They soon lost interest, however, and went back to their room to pursue other activities. I guess being younger they weren't yet bitten by the rock-and-roll bug.

After I played the song umpteen times, my mother could stand it no longer and yelled from the kitchen, "Charles Edward, will you *please* stop playing that song. I'm getting tired of hearing it." I knew she meant business when she called me by both my first and middle names. This was always a clear warning that she was on the verge of taking drastic action. I quickly obeyed her request and stopped the record in midplay. It wasn't because I really wanted to, but to prevent her from possibly confiscating my most-prized possession.

"Shake, Rattle, and Roll" was just the first of many recordings I bought during my teenage years. When the new, smaller 45-rpm vinyl plastic records were introduced, I could see they were the wave of the future and began buying my music in that format. Because our family phonograph wouldn't play 45s, I made my first major purchase: an RCA Victor 45 record changer. I kept it in my room so my sisters wouldn't mess with it. My parents were thankful that I did because they no longer had to listen to any more of "that music." Thus was born another true rock-and-roll fan. I still like some rock music — even today and at my age. And it all started one cold day on Wright Street.

The Fountain Square Record Shop was razed back in the late-1950s along with a few other businesses and homes in the area where Morris Street originally ended in a T-intersection with Shelby Street. Morris was extended via a new section that curved around behind the Fountain Square Theater Building and connected with Prospect Street. The record store was never rebuilt. The G.C. Murphy Five and Dime Store on Virginia Avenue began selling the latest 45-rpm records and became my new source for recorded music.

29

Freckles and SNO BALLS

Every weekday morning, "Big Bob" Hartman drove up in his old, black, four-door Chevy and honked the horn in front of my house. I'd run out, climb in, and take my place in the back seat. It was the first semester of my senior year and, for several months, I rode to Manual High School with Bob. I didn't really know him firsthand; he was a friend of my best buddy, Dick Foster. But this was enough to get me a spot as one of Bob's riders—as long as I paid him a buck and a half every week for gas. Dick always rode shotgun and his younger brother, John, sat in the back seat behind Bob.

We were a carload of typical teenage boys who rode together and talked about the three things teenage boys liked best: cars, sports, and girls—especially girls. We'd usually share the latest rumors or the newest dirty jokes we'd heard making the rounds at school. Once in a while we'd hold impromptu contests to see who could belch the loudest or let the biggest fart.

Dick was our uncrowned "King of Farts." I don't know what they ate at his house, but he could convert it into the most explosive, noxious gas known to man. On one memorable morning after he'd had chili for supper the night before, Dick blasted us with a discharge so foul that we had to roll down the windows and literally gasp for air. Whew! Along with our choking, we were all laughing to the point of tears. It was a real wonder this toxic emission didn't eat the fuzz off the headliner of Bob's car.

Dick's kid brother had his own specialty: burping. John was a master at it. He had such control of his oral eruptions that he could actually belch out words and, sometimes, even short expressions—usually vulgar ones. None of us could even come close to matching his performances. As boys, we all thought John's special ability to burp-talk was pure genius. It deserved and received our compliments and never failed to trigger howls of laughter.

I was no slouch in my own contributions to these crazy competitions, but I couldn't hold a candle to the Fosters. And it's a good thing no one did—it might have set off an explosion. Such shenanigans were really gross, but that's what made them so funny. Disgusting? Yes. But riding with Bob and the Foster brothers sure beat the heck out of any other way I'd gotten to high school over the years: peddling a bicycle, walking, or riding on the city bus. Now, I was traveling first-class in Big Bob's "funmobile."

One morning when I climbed into Bob's car, something was different, very different. There, sitting in the middle of the back seat, was a kind-of-cute, wide-eyed, petite "bleached blonde." Dick introduced her to me as June, a new girl who had just moved into their neighborhood. I could hardly believe she was a high schooler. She was so young and tiny that she looked like a little kid — a kid with *lots* of freckles. I couldn't help but notice, however, that she was wearing a very tight sweater — teenage boys tend to notice such things. But, unfortunately, she didn't have much "equipment" to fill out the sweater. Her knobby little boobs were so small that they looked like she was trying to hide a squashed package of Hostess Sno Balls under her clothes. I'd never been a big fan of freckles or of Sno Balls and since she was only a freshman, three years younger than me, I really wasn't attracted to her. In fact, I resented her intrusion into our gross-out gang of guys. What was Big Bob thinking? Now we'd have to watch what we said and how we acted just because a girl was on board. This was a change I definitely didn't welcome.

Just as I feared, our crazy competitions

ended immediately along with the crude jokes and course banter we'd previously enjoyed so much. Before the week was over, June had started riding up front in Dick's place. He'd been demoted to the back seat with his brother and me. Evidently, Big Bob had a special weakness for blondes—like many guys do. Or, maybe he liked Sno Balls. I guess her age and size didn't matter to him, as long as she was a blonde, even if it was produced by peroxide.

Bob and June would talk and cut up all the way to school and almost totally ignore the three of us in the back seat. June had a certain flirty way about her that brought out a whole side of Bob we'd never seen before. I couldn't help wondering if he charged her for riding like he did us. From his obvious fascination with her, my bet was that she had a free ride.

This is not quite the end of my story regarding that little blond girl I rode next to in the back seat of Bob's car for a few days. Years later, I found out from Dick that she had turned out to become the famous June Cochran. You may never have heard of her; or, if you have, you may have forgotten where. June's claim to fame resulted from becoming one of those immortals of classic beauty and pure sexuality: *a Playboy Playmate*. She was named Miss December in 1962. June must have been one of Hugh Hefner's favorites because he also chose her as Playmate of the Year for 1963. Only a select few of his bare-skinned beauties ever achieved this double distinction. There had to be a reason. Even though it was now decades later, I was dying to know what that reason was.

Today, if you Google her name and former titles on the internet, you can find June's original centerfold preserved forever in the Playboy archives. I know because I just had to check and see for myself — of course, it was done purely as "research" for writing this chapter. At least that's what I told my wife when she caught me ogling June's picture. According to her bio, June was still only 5'-2" tall at the time of her photo shoot. She may not have grown any taller over the years, but she sure had grown in other ways. And her freckles had all magically disappeared, too, thanks to the work of a very talented airbrush artist.

"Miss Freckles and Sno Balls" of 1956 now had a beautiful peaches-and-cream complexion and had somehow grown a set of jugs as big as the bumper guards on the front of a '55 Buick. Wow! All I can say is that little June Cochran sure didn't look like *that* back when we rode to Manual High School together. If she had, Big

Bob would no doubt have dumped the Foster brothers and me in a heartbeat in order to become her private chauffeur. And who would have blamed him? After all, she was a blonde.

30

Dream-Date Disaster

The Junior Prom was only a week away. I had asked a girl to go a couple of weeks back, but she was already going with another guy. So far, I hadn't gotten up the nerve to ask anyone else and by now it was way too late to do so. It looked like my fate was sealed; I wasn't going to my Junior Prom.

One morning I was in the bathroom brushing my teeth before leaving for school. I'd just started when my sister, Sandy, came up the hall and stood in the open doorway. "Got a date for the prom yet?" she asked. She knew good and well I didn't or I would've already told our whole family about it.

"Uh-uh, not goin'," I mumbled as I kept brushing.

"I know someone who'd go with you if you asked her," Sandy said with a raise of her eyebrows and a sly grin.

I spit out the toothpaste and asked, "Oh, yeah? Who would that be?"

"My friend, Zelma Stevens," Sandy said while slowly nodding her head up and down. I nearly swallowed the mouthful of water I was swishing.

I couldn't believe my ears. Zelma Stevens was one of the best-looking girls at Manual High School. She had big brown eyes, long beautiful blond hair, and a cute little beauty mark near the left corner of her mouth. She also had a body that teenage boys back then described as "really built." Yes, Zelma Stevens was an absolute dream girl — from top to bottom.

I spit out the water and asked curiously, "How's come she doesn't have a date for the prom by now? She's so pretty I thought lots of guys would be lined up to ask her to go."

"Well, she *is* a real cutie that's for sure," Sandy agreed, "but that's also her problem. I guess all the boys are thinking she's *so* cute that she must already have a date for the prom or, if not, that she'd never go with them. So, here it is only a week before the big dance and no one's asked her — and she *really* wants to go. I was talking to her yesterday and told her you didn't have a date yet either. And guess what? She said that if you'd ask her, she'd go with you."

Oh-my-gosh! This was too good to be true. A "sure thing" date with a girl who all the boys at school practically drooled over. And all I had to do was go through the formality of calling and asking her? Hmmm. I didn't have to think it over for more than a few seconds. I quickly told Sandy, "Tell Zelma I'll call her tonight. And get her phone number for me."

"Okey-dokey, I'll see her in Home Ec class this morning," Sandy replied.

I day-dreamed through most of my classes at school thinking about getting a date with Zelma. I didn't dare tell any of my friends. Maybe it would all turn out to be a joke, or maybe some other guy would ask her to the prom today at school before I called her tonight, or maybe she'd change her mind about going with me. I didn't want to blab it around and then come out looking like a fool if anything went wrong. So, it was a secret for now. Even if I had told some of my best buddies, they wouldn't have believed me — and who could blame them? After all, who would believe that the incredible Zelma Stevens would actually go to the Junior Prom with an average guy like me? I still found the idea hard to believe myself. I wasn't bad-looking and had dated several girls, so I certainly wasn't a loser. But I was way out of Zelma's league.

Sandy brought home the magic phone number that would connect me with the girl of my dreams. When she gave it to me, Sandy said everything was all set with Zelma and she was expecting my call that evening. After supper, I dialed her number. As I did, my finger almost tingled from nervous excitement in anticipation of talking one-on-one with Zelma. The phone rang a few times and someone picked it up. A very mature-sounding female voice answered, "Hello. Stevens' residence." Since I'd never spoken with Zelma on the phone before—or in person either for that matter—I thought maybe it was her mother.

"Uh, yes, could I please speak with Zelma?"

"This is Zelma," the voice purred through the receiver. She sounded as beautiful to my ears as her looks were to my eyes. I nearly melted, but pressed on with my mission. Gulping down a deep breath, I continued.

"Hi, Zelma, this is Charles White, Sandy's brother."

"Oh. Hi, Charles."

I avoided any chitchat and got right to the point. "Hey, I was wondering if you'd like to go to the Junior Prom." I quickly added, "With me."

Without hesitation, she said "Why sure. I'd *love* to go." She answered as innocently as if it hadn't been prearranged and she had no earthly idea that I was going to call and ask.

"That's great. The prom is supposed to start at 9:00, so I'll plan on picking you up around 8:30 or so. Does that sound alright?"

"Sounds good."

"O.K., then. Uh, I'd better get your address." Hastily, I wrote it down, then read it back. "Well, I'll see you Friday night, then." I'd accomplished my purpose and was way too nervous to talk any longer. I was afraid that I might say something really stupid and Zelma would change her mind about going with me.

"I'm looking forward to it," she said.

"So am I. Good-by, Zelma."

"Bye-bye, Charles."

Our conversation lasted only a minute or so, but I'd done it; I had a date with the one and only Zelma Stevens. It was a teenage boy's dream come true. Overpowered by pure joy, I was bursting to share my feelings. I found both my sisters in the bedroom they shared and told them the good news.

"Hey, guess what? I just called Zelma, and she's going to the prom with me!"

"See, I told you she would," Sandy replied with a big smile. Jackie added her congratulations. Even though she was still an eighth-grader, she'd heard from Sandy all about Zelma

Stevens and the prearranged date with me.

"Thanks for fixing me up with her. Maybe I can return the favor sometime and get you a date with one of my buddies."

"Well, I don't know about that," Sandy responded. "But I'll let you know if I ever wanna be fixed up with one of them."

I said O.K. and hurried up to my room to savor the still-fresh memories of my all-too-brief conversation with Zelma. Hadn't she said with her own sweet lips in that adorable voice of hers that she'd *love* to go with me? She could just as easily have said simply "yes" or that she'd *like* to go. But, she said she'd *love* to go. That's a powerful word to use when speaking to a teen-age boy full of hormones. My imagination told me that maybe, just maybe, Zelma really did want to go to the prom with me. My common sense, on the other hand, reminded me that her acceptance was just an act of desperation to en-sure her presence at one of the biggest social events of the school year. As it would turn out, my common sense was right and my imagina-tion was wrong. Boy, was it wrong.

While enjoying my reverie, a sudden thought struck me like a bolt of lightning — wait a minute! What an idiot; I'd forgotten one im-portant detail: how was I going to get Zelma to the prom? I didn't have a car and, on top of that, I didn't even have my driver's license yet. So, I certainly couldn't borrow the family car for the occasion. In a near panic, I wracked my brain trying to think of a solution. And, then, the answer came to me. I'd check with my good friend, Ronnie "Moose" Morris, and see if I could double-date with him. He'd told me days ago that he and Sandee, his steady girlfriend from Tech (a high school on the east side) were going to the prom.

Ronnie already had his license and had bragged proudly — and for good reason — that his older brother, Frankie, was going to let him drive his brand-new convertible to the prom. It was a two-tone blue Ford with a white top, whitewall tires, and big chrome spinner hubcaps. It even had a continental kit for the spare tire on the extended back bumper. I'd seen Frankie cruising around the neighborhood in his new Ford and heard the pulsing sound of its dual exhausted glass-pack mufflers. What a dream car.

I went downstairs and called Ronnie. He was out on a date with Sandee; I might have known he would be since it was a Friday night. When I called him again the next day, Ronnie couldn't believe it when I told him that I actually had a date for the prom with Zelma Stevens. That was the good news. Then for the bad news: I had no way to get her there other than by taxi or my dad driving us. Neither option was a good idea when you had a date with a hot number like Zelma. Ronnie immediately sympathized with my predicament. Before I could even ask him, he asked me if I wanted to double-date with him and Sandee. What a pal. I thanked him for getting me out of the jam I was in and told him I'd pay for the gas. He said not to worry about it (gasoline was only about 25 cents a gallon back then).

As I tried to go to sleep that night, I felt happier than I'd ever been in my life. Imagine, me taking Zelma Stevens to the Junior Prom, and riding in a cool new convertible. I could see it all in my mind; it would be an absolute dream date with a dream girl in a dream car. I was far too optimistic at the moment to realize that such dreams don't always come true.

The week of the prom was a busy one. I bought our tickets at school on Monday. On Tuesday after school, Dad took me uptown to Skeffington's Formal Wear Shop so I could be measured and order a tuxedo. Ordering Zelma's corsage presented its own challenges. I didn't know what color her dress would be or if it was strapless or had straps. Sandy suggested I order a wrist corsage made of white flowers, so it would go with any color or type of dress. Since I wanted to go all-out and get something befitting this extra-special occasion, I ordered the most expensive flowers available: miniature white orchids. The florist said they would include a complimentary boutonnière for me. Perfect. I ordered them despite the cost. Zelma was worth it.

The week flew by and soon Friday arrived. Dad drove me back to Skeffington's to pick up my tux. Zelma's flowers were delivered as ordered. After bathing and washing my hair, I brushed my flattop so it looked just right. I hadn't started shaving yet, but I did splash on some of Dad's aftershave lotion just to give the impression that I had shaved. Then I put on my white ruffle-front shirt and my fancy black tux. The pants were a little long, but I hiked up the suspenders and that solved the problem. I got the corsage box from the fridge and was all set to go when Ronnie and Sandee pulled up in front. As planned, they were in Frankie's Ford. I'd been afraid something would happen at the last minute to keep Ronnie from being able to borrow it. But I needn't have worried; there they sat in that beautiful convertible. What a perfect spring evening; just warm enough that having the top down felt good. I jumped in, said "hi" to Ronnie and Sandee, told him Zelma's address, and off we went. My dream date was underway.

Ronnie headed out Morris Street into the southwest part of town. My anticipation and nervousness grew the closer we came to Zelma's. We soon turned onto her street and Ronnie pulled up in front of a house on a corner. "Here it is," he said. I couldn't believe my eyes. The place was dilapidated and needed painting. There was hardly a blade of grass in the entire yard; it was mostly just bare dirt. Was *this* the right address? I checked the house numbers again. It was.

I climbed out of the back seat and walked over to the gateway in the rusty wire fence. The gate was half off its hinges and hanging open. I carefully walked across the yard on a couple of wide wooden boards that served as a walkway. Was this place for real? As I knocked on the rickety screen door, the scary thought occurred to me that maybe this was all just a cruel joke and Zelma had given me a phony address with no intention of really going to the prom with me. A woman with a cigarette in her mouth came to the door. I asked her, "Is this the Stevens residence?" I almost hoped it wasn't.

"It sure is, young man. You come right on in here." She attempted to wave the hovering cloud of cigarette smoke away as I entered. Zelma's parents introduced themselves while the family dog sniffed at my rented patent leather shoes. I shook hands with her dad. He was in his undershirt, and not a very clean one at that. Mrs. Stevens said that Zelma was just about ready. I didn't even have time to sit down before into the room she came.

I could barely believe my eyes; Zelma was absolutely stunning. Her long golden hair hung straight down to her shoulders. She was wearing a pale orange chiffon, strapless, floor-length gown that hugged every curve in her body. Her long necklace of tiny white pearls hung low enough to draw attention to the fact that she was "stacked" (as boys used to say back then of girls with well-developed breasts). She looked at me with those big brown eyes through her long mascared eyelashes and said two words: "Hi, Charles." I was speechless. Suddenly, it didn't matter that her yard had no grass, or that her screen door was loose, or that her father wasn't a snappy dresser.

As we stood there awkwardly, she spotted the corsage box in my hand and asked,

"What's that?" I was still gaga at this point, but managed to say, "Oh, it's flowers I got for you." I took the corsage out of the box and slipped the elastic strap around her delicate wrist as she extended it toward me. "They're *orchids*," I said proudly. Her eyes sparkled as she said, "Thank you, Charles. I love them." There was that magic word again. When I heard it, I was really glad that I hadn't ordered the cheaper carnations.

Then I handed her my boutonnière. We stood there practically toe to toe while she pinned the flower on my lapel. As she fumbled with the long pin, I inhaled her perfume deeply. The fragrance reminded me of Cashmere Bouquet soap. It smelled divine. I tried not to look down into her cleavage, but dared a quick glance while she was still pinning on my flower. Mmm-mmm! I didn't know it at the time, but this was as close as I was going to get to Zelma all evening.

Mrs. Stevens came over to take a closer look at Zelma's corsage. "Them sure are some real fancy flowers. Zell, honey, they go just perfect with yer new dress." Then, looking toward me, her mother asked, "Don't she look purty?" It was a question that needed no answer, but I answered anyway.

"She sure does," I replied enthusiastically.

Zelma looked over at me, rolled her eyes, and smiled in an awkward way. I could sense her embarrassment as she said, "Well, I guess we better be going, Charles."

I told her folks it was nice meeting them and we said our good-byes. Her mom said, "Y'uns have a real good time." Her dad said that, since it was a prom and lasted till midnight, Zelma could stay out till one-thirty, but no later. I promised to have her home on time. Carefully opening the screen door, I held it open for her as we left.

Taking Zelma's soft, warm hand in mine, I steadied her as she tottered along the board walkway in her high heels. She had to lift the hem of her gown slightly to keep it from dragging and snagging on the rough planks. When we got to the gateway, I helped her down the two steps to the sidewalk. Before taking the steps, she lifted her dress a little higher and exposed her shapely ankles and lower calves. They were just as perfect as the rest of her.

I didn't want to let go of Zelma's hand after I'd helped her into the back seat, but forced myself. After she was seated, I introduced her to Ronnie and Sandee. Zelma commented about the nice car Ronnie was driving. He smiled proudly and said it was his brother's. With the intros over, Ronnie fired up the Ford and away we went. My dream was coming true — or so it seemed.

On our way to the prom, Zelma wasn't very talkative. I hoped it was because we were in the back seat of a convertible and the wind made it difficult to carry on a conversation. The fact that she didn't know Ronnie or Sandee may also have been a factor. About the only thing Zelma said was to ask Ronnie if he'd mind raising the top because the wind was messing up her hair. He complied out of politeness, but I don't think he really wanted to. Even with the top up, Zelma still wouldn't say much. I wasn't the greatest conversationalist myself, so we had a pretty quiet time in the back seat. I was just glad to be sitting next to her, even if she wouldn't make any small talk. We listened to the radio and said next to nothing. Ronnie and Sandee chatted back and forth and asked us an occasional question in an attempt to break up the awkward silence. Their well-meant effort was wasted.

Ronnie parked in a garage and we walked the block or two to the Indiana Roof Ballroom. This was a super fancy place with twinkling lights in the ceiling and indirect lighting around the walls. There was a big stage with spotlights for the live band and lots of cozy little round tables to sit at. All the dances I'd been to previously had been held in the school cafeteria; the ballroom was quite a step up. Once inside, we found a table and ordered a round of Cokes. Only soft drinks and punch were available and no one tried to sneak in any "hard stuff." In those days, most teens didn't drink alcohol. Besides, the dance was heavily chaperoned by adults just in case anyone would have tried something out of line.

Did I mention that I couldn't dance worth a hoot? Although I could fake my way through a slow number, when it came to the fast stuff, I was lost. As it turned out, it didn't matter much because Zelma and I never danced — not even once — during the entire evening. I asked her if she wanted to during a couple of slower-paced songs, but she wasn't interested. I thought maybe she was like me and didn't know how to dance, but I'll bet she could have if she'd really wanted to. As Zelma and I sat at the table, there was very little conversation between us. If I asked her a question, she'd answer me in as few words as possible and then clam up again. Things were definitely *not* going according to my dream.

After half an hour of this and acting more

and more bored by the minute, Zelma excused herself and said she was going to go talk to some of her girl friends. She obviously wanted to circulate in order to be seen by everyone. Unfortunately, she didn't want to be seen with me. I kept an eye on her as she moved around from one table to another, laughing and chatting with her friends and their dates. None of the other boys asked her to dance; they were all there with their own dates and wouldn't dare—even if they had gotten up the nerve.

Time dragged by. I started walking around and gabbing with some of my buddies. As predicted, they could hardly believe that I was really there with Zelma Stevens. As it turned out, "with" was a very relative term. We came together and left together, but were hardly with one another all evening.

Ronnie and Sandee had a hi-o time dancing nearly every dance and chatting away like the lovebirds they were. They held hands and even sneaked a kiss now and then, but that's as far as it went. Public displays of affection weren't socially acceptable back then. How I envied Ronnie. Here I was on a date with one of the most beautiful girls in our school, and she'd barely give me the time of day.

Finally, the last dance was danced—but

not by us — and Manual's 1956 Junior Prom was history. We mixed in with the other couples as everyone converged on the elevators and rode them down jammed in like sardines. Zelma managed to avoid standing next to me on the elevator and stood over in the corner. As we got off and left the lobby, Zelma was quiet again, except when she waved and yelled good-byes to her girl friends she spotted in the crowd.

On our way back to the parking garage, Ronnie and Sandee were holding hands and laughing as Zelma and I walked along behind them like we didn't even know each other. Zelma slipped off her heels and walked bare-foot down the wide sidewalk. She stopped and glanced at a few store window displays along the way, but didn't say a word to me.

Back at the garage, we climbed into the car. I offered Zelma my hand to assist her, but she wouldn't take it. The opening-closing mechanism for the convertible top took about six inches off each end of the back seat, so it was narrower than the front seat. Zelma sat as far away from me as she possibly could. Ronnie had his arm around Sandee up in front, but it was immediately obvious that there would be no hanky-panky of any kind in the back. By this time, it came as no surprise.

Since it was only a little after midnight, Ronnie suggested that we head for the Tee-Pee or the Southern Circle (two of the most popular drive-in hangouts for Manual students) and get something to eat. Zelma, however, she said she wasn't hungry and didn't want to go. "Just take me home," she requested sharply. Oh, boy. It was obvious that our date was over and there was no need to prolong our mutual misery any longer. At least I wouldn't have to waste any more money on her. All of us were quiet as Ronnie drove back to Zelma's. The music on the radio provided the only diversion from the uncomfortable silence.

Ronnie pulled up in front of Zelma's and turned off the engine. My watch said it wasn't even 12:30 — a whole hour before her curfew. I'd thought back over the entire evening on our way to her house and I was thoroughly p.o.'d by then. I opened the car door and climbed out. Zelma followed on her own with my assistance neither asked for nor offered. I knew what manners were, but made no move toward escorting her to the front door. Since her porch light was on and there was a bright street light on the corner, she could easily see her way across the yard. Besides, it was quite obvious by now that she didn't want me to walk her up to the door and have to go through any awkward parting.

Still barefoot and carrying her heels, Zelma went up the steps and crossed the board walkway. No "thank-you," no "good-by." *Nothing.* I stood there numbly watching her walk out of my shattered dream. Just before she reached her front door, I had to say something. I yelled out—facetiously, of course—"Hope you had a nice time." Under my breath, I said to myself, "I sure didn't." Zelma had to have heard me, but she went inside without making a response or even looking back.

I slid into the front seat with Ronnie and Sandee, slammed the door, and took off my bow tie. "Man, I bet you're glad that's over," he said. All I could say at the moment was simply, "Yeah." They asked me if I wanted to go get something to eat. "Sure, why not?" I replied, "I'm starved." Before we left, Ronnie took a minute to lower the top. While he did, I unpinned my boutonnière and tossed it on the sidewalk in front of the steps up into Zelma's yard. I hoped she'd find it lying there wilted and dead like my dream date turned out. As we pulled away, Ronnie kicked the gas and blasted the Ford's duals in a parting "tribute."

It was great to be with friends who liked me and actually carried on real conversation.

They couldn't get over how rudely Zelma had acted all evening and the crappy way she'd treated me. Maybe I should've expected it under the circumstances. I guess my over-optimistic teenage dream had blinded me to the *real* reason why Zelma went as my date to the prom. But now the dream was over and I was wide awake. The cool air felt good as we drove into the night in search of a cheeseburger.

The Indiana Roof Ballroom on the sixth floor of the Indiana Theater Building at 140 W. Washington Street is still open and in active use for dances and other social functions. The Tee Pee Restaurant on Madison Avenue was razed several years ago and replaced with a McDonald's. The Southern Circle Restaurant "way out in the country" on U.S. 31 was torn down (around the time the Southern Plaza Shopping Center was constructed in the early 1960s) and replaced with the Dutch Oven Restaurant, followed by a succession of other eating places over the years on the same property. It is now part of the shopping center parking lot.

Photographs

**Front view of author's house at 1218 Wright Street.
Looks like hedges were due for trimming by Dad.
Note unusual square tower on house next door.**

**Author (age 8-1/2) with sisters Jacqueline Sue (age 4-1/2)
and Sandra Lee (age 6) out in front of their house.**

**Author at age 10
(when I was a flag boy).**

**Author at age 11
(nice tie, huh?).**

**Author at age 12
(my "weasel" look).**

**Author at age 18
(loved that flattop haircut).**

Our two pet squirrels Pit and Pat
(or is it Pat and Pit?--always hard to tell them apart).

Author (age 18) surrounded by sister Sandy (16)
on left, sister Jackie (14) in front, and Joyce (17) my high
school sweetheart (and eventually my wife) on Easter
Sunday 1957 in front of our house on Wright Street.

Appendices

Appendix A

The White House

I had the privilege of growing up in the White house. No, not the world-famous one at 1600 Pennsylvania Avenue in Washington. My White house was located at 1218 Wright Street in Indianapolis and was a far less imposing structure. It was a modest frame bungalow sitting on a typical 25-foot wide city lot. Like most houses on our street, ours covered nearly the entire lot width. There was just enough room for a sidewalk that ran along the entire south side of our house. Since we were located in the middle of the block, our north property line abutted a paved alley. The front of the White house was dominated by a wide concrete-floored, screened-in porch with red brick pillars and railing walls. Most houses in the neighborhood had porches, but very few were screened. Ours was by far the largest of them all.

The White house was painted white, the most common color for houses in those days.

The house was roofed with green roll roofing, a cheaper alternative to shingles. The porch, however, was roofed with unusual six-sided green shingles. The face of a large front gable above the porch was decorated with several overlapping rows of decorative wooden shingles. These had rounded ends and looked something like large fish scales from a distance. Centered in the gable was a group of three small attic windows. The larger center window pane was surrounded by a three-inch band of red glass rectangles with blue glass squares at each corner. Several other houses along our street also had windows with the added fancy touch of colored glass. Unfortunately, when Dad had the house painted one summer, the painters covered over all three of the gable windows—colored glass and all. I'll never understand why.

A thick waist-high hedge bordered the front yard and extended down our south property line along the walk on that side of our house. The hedge also ran along the edge of the alley from the front walk to the front corner of our house. Chainlink fencing ran along both side property lines in our backyard from the house out to our garage.

We had no trees in the front yard, but we were lucky. Our next-door neighbors, the

Manns, had a large one growing near our common property line. This tree shaded more of our yard and porch than it did of theirs. My two sisters and I often played in the shade of that tree, but had to constantly be on watch for the half-inch long black ants that had a nest nearby. Our backyard had two trees taller than the house. One stood on either side of a narrow concrete walk running straight down the middle of our yard. These trees shaded our back porch and nearly half of the yard for part of the day.

Mom usually planted a small vegetable garden in the backyard each summer. Nothing fancy. Just a few radishes, carrots, and maybe some lettuce. She also enjoyed growing flowers. Mom was proud of the large bed of lilies-of-the-valley she grew outside her front bedroom window. These tiny white, bell-shaped flowers had a sweet fragrance noticeable by anyone coming within a few feet of them. Since that side of the house was in shade most of the day, several ferns grew adjacent to the flower bed.

Mom kept a triangular-shaped bed of yellow and lavender irises growing between the walk and the hedge at the back corner of our house. Some summers, she planted blue and white morning glories along the width of our back porch. These provided shade from the morning sun and served as a privacy screen from what little traffic there was in our alley. As they grew, these climbers twined their way around strings that Dad ran from the ground up to the beam running between the porch roof pillars.

At the far back of our property stood an old wooden building. It must have originally been a one-stall stable (now our storage shed) and a carriage house (now our garage). Like our house, the garage-shed was painted white. The roof was covered with black roll roofing. This building was not wired for electricity, so had no lights. The shed floor was rough concrete; the garage floor was just packed dirt. Inside the garage you could smell the motor oil that had been drained out of cars through the years and disposed of by being spread over the dirt floor. Two large, hinged wooden doors swung out from the alley end of the garage. An access door into the garage from the yard was located near the opposite end. A similar door stood beside it and opened into the shed. Once in awhile, my sisters and I played in the garage. Our mother didn't especially like this. She was afraid we'd track oily dirt into the house. We always made sure to wipe our feet off good in the grass so this wouldn't happen.

When entering our house, you first came through the screened-in front porch. Dad had an annual ritual of bringing the wooden-framed screens out of storage in the shed. I'd help him hose them off, clean them thoroughly with a scrub brush and bucket of suds, and then rinse them with the hose. The porch had been custom-built, so the screens weren't all interchangeable. Dad found a clever system for getting the correct screen in each opening. He bought a set of special marker nails at the hardware store and drove one in the bottom of each screen frame. Each nail head bore a number. The matching opening on the porch received a nail with the duplicate number. This system was much simpler than the trial-and-error process we originally had to go through each spring.

When autumn came, Dad took down the screens—always before Halloween, so no neighborhood tricksters would soap them. One year it stayed warm longer than usual and we were a little late taking down the screens. And don't you know, a Halloween prankster came around a few days before the big night and soaped all the screens on the front of the porch. Dad was really ticked off about it. Guess who got the job of taking the screens down and cleaning them?

From then on, as long as I was still living at home, I made sure the screens came down early in October—regardless of the temperature.

Adjacent to the screened porch was a cozy sun porch about six by ten feet. The porch floor was concrete, painted gray, and nearly covered by a sheet of flowery linoleum. Three square windows lined the outside wall; the center window was screened and swung open for ventilation in the summer. The upper half of the porch entry door was glass and had a window on each side. The two outside walls were brick halfway up with the windows above them. The two inside walls were covered with wood siding like the rest of the house's exterior. All these walls were painted gray like the porch floor.

The sun porch was our favorite place to play or read on rainy or cool days and in the winter when we couldn't play outside. Two big comfy chairs and an odd piece of wooden furniture called a "hall tree" occupied most of the porch space. The hall tree was sort of a fancy coat rack with a wide boxlike base seat that had an arm at each end. My sisters and I stored our comics, other books, and a few of our favorite games in a large storage compartment under the seat's lid. A rectangular mirror was built into the tree's high back. Two ornate metal hooks were mounted on each side of the mirror for hanging hats and coats, but they were seldom used for their intended purpose. An old umbrella hung permanently hung on one of the hooks.

The inner sun porch door opened into our living room. Originally, it had opened into the room that was probably called the parlor. This room became a bedroom shared by my two sisters. To eliminate the awkward traffic pattern, our father hired a carpenter to relocate the entrance so that it came into what had once been the dining room, but which was our living room. We ate all our meals in the kitchen and didn't need a formal dining room. The living room was about twelve feet square and had a set of three small windows up high along the outside wall. Along the bottom edge of these windows ran a wide shelf on which Mom displayed family photos and a few knickknacks. The living room walls were covered with a pink and beige-colored, bumpy textured wallpaper. A large brown area rug covered the floor nearly wall-to-wall. The living room had doors on three walls opening into my sisters' bedroom, our parents' bedroom, and the kitchen.

My sisters shared the front bedroom. It had three large windows as tall as doorways, two of which opened out onto the front porch. They could, therefore, be left open in warm weather with no fear of it raining in. Since this room was originally the parlor, it lacked a closet. So, Sandy and Jackie shared a wooden wardrobe for their clothes. Their room was decorated with girlish flowered wallpaper. One wall contained a fireplace that long ago had been bricked up and covered over. Only the mantel survived. It was used as a display shelf for my sisters' small collection of Storybook Dolls. Since this was a good-sized room (maybe twelve feet square), the girls had plenty of space for their beds, dressers, chairs, and toys.

The other downstairs bedroom was the one used by my parents. This room was fairly small for a master bedroom, being only about ten feet square. The limited wall space contained the entry door (originally a large archway), two tall windows, a small closet, and a door into the bathroom. The walk-in closets in most modern homes today are bigger than this bedroom was. The room was nearly filled with furniture: a double bed, nightstand, dresser, and my mother's vanity with a large round mirror attached. This room was wallpapered with a pattern of vines and flowers. Two framed pictures of multicolored parrots hung above the bed to provide some decoration.

Adjacent to our parents' bedroom was our house's only bathroom. The bath had one door opening off their bedroom and another door opening onto a short hallway to the kitchen. Five of us shared the bathroom and, somehow, we all managed to survive. I remember very few times having any "scheduling difficulties" for the use of the toilet — even if the seat was often still warm from the previous user. Hey, in the winter this was a real plus.

Our bathroom had no exhaust fan, but it did have a two-foot square window on the alleyside wall which could be swung open (weather permitting) for ventilation. The window was set high in the wall, so there was no way that persons walking down the alley could sneak any peeks on their way by.

When we moved into our house, the bathroom still had its original free-standing clawfoot bathtub, as did most homes in those days. Dad later hired a carpenter to box the tub in with a wooden frame. During this remodel, the bathroom walls and the new tub enclosure were covered with pale yellow linoleum patterned to look like ceramic tile. This didn't fool anyone, but did give the old tub a much more "modern" look.

A large built-in corner cabinet extended from floor to ceiling and provided plenty of space for all our toiletries, towels, and other bathroom items. Our small wall-mounted sink had no countertop or surround on which to sit anything. The hot and cold water faucets didn't even match; the hot was the original old brass and the cold was a newer chrome. By today's standards, our bathroom would be considered a complete redo. But, for the five of us, it served its purpose well. The need for a second bathroom was never even considered. Where would we have put one?

Our kitchen was spacious enough to accommodate a table and six chairs in the center of the room. A white porcelain double sink with draining boards on each end occupied most of the outside wall. Two large side-by-side windows over the sink extended nearly to the ceiling. The kitchen had six doors—more than any other room in the house. There was a door out into the rumpus room on the back of the house, a basement door, a door into a walk-in pantry, a doorway into the hall, another doorway into the living room, and a door opening out onto the walk that ran along the side of the house. Our milkbox (provided by Roberts Dairy) sat next to the steps outside this door.

The upper kitchen walls were painted a bright, cheerful yellow with a shiny finish that was easy to wipe off. The lower part of the walls were covered with tongue-and-groove paneling about waist-high on an adult. This and all other woodwork in the room was painted a light cream color. The floors were covered with linoleum: black with a pattern of white speckles.

Our gas stove was located on the west wall and our Frigidaire stood on the east wall. Mom's trusty old pedal-operated Singer sewing machine sat in the northeast corner. Our kitchen had only two cabinets, but they were really big ones extending from floor to ceiling. One was a glass-doored china cabinet built into the east wall; the other was a large corner cabinet at the right end of the sink housing all Mom's baking and cooking utensils and supplies.

As in most modern homes, our kitchen was the center of activity in our house on Wright Street. The girls did their homework at the kitchen table since they didn't have a desk in their room like I did. The family gathered around the same table for supper each evening. Mom used the table to lay out material she was working on while making clothes for her and my sisters. Dad would often put the table to good use as a workbench for his home repair projects. Whenever the family played games together, the kitchen table also served as our game table. It was here that Dad taught me how to play and win at checkers. Our family birthday parties were all held in the kitchen around this well-worn, but sturdy, wooden table.

Off the kitchen in the center of the north wall between the hallway and the basement door was a large walk-in pantry about four feet wide by seven feet long. The pantry was walled with tongue-and-groove boards. The back and one side wall were lined with shelves. Off-season and seldom-used items were stored here, along with all Dad's show business equipment. He also kept all his tools on one of the shelves so they'd be handy when he needed them. Since this shelf always seemed messy, I took great pride in organizing his tools and hanging them on the wall so he could find them easier. Dad was surprised by my doing this and really appreciated it.

After we lived on Wright Street for a few years, Dad and Mom turned the back room off the kitchen into what we called the "rumpus room." This space was originally used only for storage and as a catch-all area. Our parents converted it into the 1940s equivalent of a small family room. The rumpus room had three windows, each about thirty inches square. Two of these opened under our back porch, so they could be left open even during rainstorms to let fresh air into the house. Remember, we had *no* air-conditioning in those days. The only air we got was what blew in through open windows — if and when the wind blew.

Our rumpus room had a long wooden bar across one end. Dad built it himself and was quite proud of it. He equipped it with four used bar stools he bought at a restaurant supply store. Behind the bar, stood an old Coca-Cola cooler. This was a nonelectric model that used ice to chill drinks (which weren't always Cokes). Dad kept his "adult beverages" behind the bar. We kids were never allowed to go back there on pain of getting the strap.

Dad also bought a sturdy card and game table with four chairs for the other end of the room. A single bed was lined up along one wall and was supplied with several throw pillows for use as a couch to flop on. During the summer, I usually slept on this bed because the rumpus room was a little cooler at night than my regular bedroom upstairs under its uninsulated roof. My sister and I and our friends spent many happy hours in our rumpus room playing magnetic pick-up sticks, Old Maid, Parcheesi, Chinese checkers, dominoes, and other games. We were the only kids in the neighborhood we knew of who had such a special room just to play and have fun in.

The back half of our house had a basement under it; the rest of the house had only a crawl space. The basement had been dug years after the house was built when one of the previous owners decided to put in a coal furnace. The basement was nothing fancy; it had concrete block walls and a concrete floor. Our basement contained the huge furnace and stoker unit, a gas water heater, Mom's electric wringer-type washer, and the odds and ends found in most basements. The front corner on the alley side was occupied by our coal bin which was partitioned off with some old wooden doors. The distinct odor of the coal always gave our basement a unique smell. This was most noticeable after we received a fresh load hand-shoveled through our coal chute from a dump truck parked in the alley.

A concrete stairway up to the backyard occupied the other corner of the basement on the alley side. These stairs were used primarily for taking out metal tubs of ashes from our furnace. The tubs were then set out in the alley for pickup by the trash men. After becoming a teenager, one of my chores during heating season was to perform this onerous task. It's a wonder I didn't end up with a double hernia. Man, those tubs were heavy.

Mom was a big believer in home canning, so she kept lots and lots of canning and jelly jars of all sizes in the basement. The empty ones were stored in boxes up on a wide ledge that ran shoulder-high around the back and south sides of the basement wall. Mom also used this ledge to display her inventory of various jellies, jams, and other foods she had canned. Lots of yummy eating came out of those jars.

Mom didn't have a clothes dryer until several years after we moved into our house on Wright Street, so she dried everything on clotheslines. Dad strung several lengths of rope back and forth across the width of the basement for this purpose. In nice weather, Mom might hang a few things outside. But she had strong feelings that it wasn't proper to have your family's underwear flapping in the breeze for all the world to see. As a result, these "unseeables" were always dried down in our basement.

Upstairs, running the full length of the house (not including the front and back porches or the rumpus room), was my bedroom and an unfinished attic storage area. My room occupied about two-thirds of this space and had one window at the end facing the backyard. In those days, houses weren't insulated. Consequently, my room was really cold in the winter and really hot in the summer. And I mean *really*. Except for these uncomfortable times, I enjoyed having one of the best rooms a boy could possibly have. It is described in detail in Appendix B, titled "In My Room."

The White house I grew up in may have lacked all the amenities that are most desireable to today's demanding home buyers, but it had several unique features that even many modern homes lack. As I think back, there wasn't another house on all of Wright Street that I would rather have grown up in than the one at 1218.

Appendix B

In My Room

There were certain advantages to being the only boy in our family. One of them was having my own bedroom. My two sisters had to share a room and they were always a little jealous of the large one that I enjoyed all to myself. Who could blame them? My bedroom *was* big. It was upstairs and extended over most of the first floor of our house. This made my room as large as some efficiency apartments. The only minor disadvantage was that I had to run downstairs to reach our only bathroom.

My room was reached by going to the end of the short hall off the kitchen, turning left, climbing a short flight of four steps, turning left again at the stairway landing, then continuing up a long flight of twelve more steps. These uncarpeted wooden stairs were painted dark brown. The floor in my room was covered with inlaid linoleum in a tan corklike pattern.

After my parents heard me up and walking around my room in the middle of the night a couple of times, they questioned me about it and figured out that I was occasionally sleep-walking. As a safety precaution, Dad made a sturdy wooden gate and mounted it on hinges so it would swing across the top of the stair-way. Part of my nightly going-to-bed ritual was closing and latching this gate. My sleep-walk-ing was infrequent, but I was thankful for my parents' concern and for the added security they provided.

The ceiling of my room was directly un-der our house's roof. Therefore, it had two slop-ing sides which were separated by a flat strip about eighteen inches wide running down the middle of the ceiling between them. The side walls of my room were only four feet tall, but the room was large enough that I still had plenty of space to move around without bumping my head on the sloping ceiling sections. The walls and ceiling were wallpapered in a pattern that looked like knotty pine boards — complete with the knots. This gave my room a cozy cabin-like feel.

I decorated the ceiling of my room with colorful pennants from the state parks and other special places we visited as a family. I had a few others supposedly from famous federal prisons, but they were actually just fun items I bought in a novelty shop. Along with these, I had a pirate flag. I'd become fascinated by pirates since first reading about them as a young boy participating in the Public Library's summer reading program. When I saw that Jolly Roger flag with its gruesome skull grinning at me from over a pair of crossed bones, I had to have it. My ceiling also provided plenty of space to display a collection of road maps, including a large one of the entire USA, plus smaller ones of Indiana and several Midwestern states.

My room had only one window. It was at the end of my room facing the backyard and was about thirty inches wide by five feet tall. Dad bought two sliding screens that allowed keeping the window open for fresh air. One was a wooden screen about eighteen inches tall; the other screen was only about nine inches tall, but had a metal cover with louvers that allowed keeping the window open even when it was raining. Later, Dad bought a used window fan to help keep my room, and the rest of the house, a little cooler during the summer months. "Cooler" was only a relative term at best in those days of no insulation and no air-conditioning. The fan helped some, but when I ran it on high was as noisy as an old airplane engine with a propellor.

A dark green roller shade was mounted

above the window. Over the blind hung a set of heavy cotton curtains woven in a pattern of small orange, green, brown, and white squares. The combination of the blind and the curtains helped keep my room fairly dark. This was a good thing since I was a sleeper who preferred total darkness.

At the front end of my room was a door opening into an unfinished attic used for storage. The first night I slept up in my bedroom all by myself, I thought I could hear that door open and I heard the floor creak. I laid there terrified that "something" horrible was coming out of that dark, scary, cobweb-filled attic to get me. Nothing ever did, of course. I was only about five at the time and, like many five-year olds, I had a vivid imagination. I wasn't afraid of the dark, just fearful of what I thought might be *in* the dark. My parents solved this problem by finding an old skeleton key and locking the attic door. That ended my fears about "attic monsters."

As I grew older and started collecting things that boys like to collect, I mounted a set of miniature license plates down the center of the attic door. Around the door frame, I put up a sizable collection of automobile logos, each about the size of a coaster. These much-desired items were obtained by saving cereal box tops and sending in the required number with a small cash amount for shipping and handling. I was really proud of these collections. The door and frame were perfect places to display them.

The northeast corner of my room next to the attic door was occupied by an unusual triangular-shaped walk-in closet. It wasn't huge, but it was roomy enough for me to keep all my clothes and most of my toys and other stuff. The closet had a regular-size door that swung outward. Inside were several shelves built into the two side corners of the triangle. A strong clothes rod made from a length of iron pipe ran from one wall to the other across the back of the closet. Keeping my closet organized was probably where I got started toward becoming a "neat freak."

I decorated the long front closet wall with some large, full-color prints of classic World War II aircraft. These were issued during the war by the Coca-Cola Company for use in advertising their popular drink. My father knew someone who worked for Coke and was able to get two series of ten pictures each just for me. Those twenty dramatic pictures started my life-long fascination with airplanes — especially ones from the days of WW II. These included the P-

38 "Lightning," the P-39 "Airacobra," the P-47 "Thunderbolt," the P-51 "Mustang," and the P-61 "Black Widow." How could a boy *not* fall in love with airplanes having exciting names like these?

The only other noteworthy feature of my room was a cast-iron pipe that ran from the floor up through one side of the sloping ceiling. The pipe was five inches in diameter and functioned as the vent line for the toilet in our bathroom downstairs. Every time someone flushed the commode, the noise of the water refilling the tank echoed up through this pipe. I soon got used to it. For some reason, this pipe was painted an odd shade of green, so odd, in fact, that I've never seen a color exactly like it since. The pipe was out of the way, although I did manage to run into it once during one of my occasional sleepwalking rambles. I woke up immediately, fortunately without injury.

I was lucky to have a full-size bed all for myself. Standing beside the bed was a table that my Uncle Charles (my mother's brother and my namesake) made especially for me, his only nephew. His hobby was woodworking and he was highly skilled at it. The table had an eight-sided top, four sturdy square legs with cross braces forming a shelf, and was stained a dark walnut brown.

Sitting on the table was a unique wooden lamp also made by my talented uncle. The lamp was shaped like Pluto, the popular Walt Disney cartoon character. Pluto's tongue was cut from a piece of textured red leather and his tail was made from a piece of coat-hanger wire. The lamp was painted in authentic colors and was turned on and off by twisting a button-type switch that Uncle Chuck had cleverly built into Pluto's nose. This special lamp made me the envy of my friends. You couldn't buy a lamp like mine; it was truly one-of-a-kind. I wish I still had it.

Other furniture in my room included a wooden straight-back chair and a dresser (both painted in that odd green), and a tall metal cabinet with shelves in which to store my shoes. Somehow, the cabinet escaped being painted green like nearly everything else was and retained its original pale yellow color. Eventually, when my parents bought a new living room suite, I inherited the old couch and chair for my room. They were still in decent shape and fit perfectly in the spaces available. This gives you some idea of the generous size of my bedroom.

In the northwest corner of the room, my father built me a sturdy workbench from two

12-inch wide boards about six feet long. Dad bought me a small vise to hold projects and a set of tools of my very own. I hung my tool collection on the wall just above the bench. I learned at an early to have a place for everything and to keep everything in its place. I've tried to practice that principle throughout my life by always keeping things neat and well-organized.

After I turned twelve, got a paper route, and started making money, I purchased an unfinished desk and a two-shelf bookcase. Dad helped me paint them. Guess what color? Yep, more of that crazy green. My folks must have had a gallon of it stashed somewhere. You might think it would've dried up by then. Maybe it did and they bought more to match the existing items already painted that odd color.

In my mind's eye, I can still clearly remember every detail of my boyhood bedroom. If I could somehow return and spend even a few minutes there, I'd go in a heartbeat. Unfortunately, that room, like the rest of my family's house on Wright Street, now exists only in my memories of the countless happy hours I spent there — both alone and with my various friends — over the years. And, yes, my room also exists in that one not-so-happy memory of the night an indescribable "thing" staggered out of the attic to get me. What an imagination. What a room.

Appendix C

Big Things That Came Along
While I Was Growing Up

Here's a list (far from comprehensive) of some historical events, new inventions, outstanding personalities, and other "big things" that burst onto the scene while I was growing up on Wright Street in Indianapolis back in the 1940s and '50s. These will be familiar to readers from that era. Others may have never heard of many of these things except in history books.

Alaska and Hawaii admitted as the 49th and 50th states. Atomic bombs. Ball-point pens. Bubble gum. Calculators. Cinemascope. Cinerama. Civil Defense. Clackers. Communism. Contact lenses. Customized cars. Elvis Presley. End of WWII. Flat-top haircuts (guys). Guided missiles. Hardtop convertibles. Hula Hoops. "I Like Ike." I Love Lucy. Korean War. M & Ms. Mexican jumping beans. Moon discs (auto hub caps). Nuclear power. Penicillin. Pet chameleons. Pink and black clothing. Poodle hair cuts (gals). Push-button phones. Rock &

Roll. Saddle shoes (gals). Blue suede shoes (guys). Television. The Beatles. Transistor radios. 3-D movies (with special glasses). 10-speed bikes.

Appendix D

Old Things That Have Disappeared Since I Grew Up

This is a list of things that have totally or nearly disappeared since I was a kid growing up on Wright Street in Indianapolis back in the 1940s and '50s. Most of these will not be familiar to younger readers. Other readers may remember some of these, or remember hearing about them from older people. Names shown in boldface type were specific to Indianapolis.

A & P Groceries. Air-Wick air freshener. Alley Oop. Angora collars. Ankle bracelets. Arbor Day observances. Artificial poppies worn on Veterans' Day (a.k.a. Armistice Day). Ayds diet candy. **Ayr-Way Discount Stores.**

Ban-Lon sweaters. Beanies. Big bands. Bi-wing airplanes. Black and white movies. Black armbands to denote people in mourning. Blackboards. Black wreaths on doors to denote households in mourning. Breadmen. Breeze soap powder. Bromo-seltzer. Buddha-shaped

305

incense burners. Burlesque. Burma Shave signs along highways. Bermuda bells on cars.

Campaign buttons. Canaries. Cap guns. "CASH & CARRY" signs in stores. Cashmere Bouquest soap. Charlie McCarthy. Charm bracelets. Christmas carolers. Church bells ringing. Circus posters. City-wide annual "Clean up-Paint up-Fix up" campaigns (in the spring). Clinkers. Classics Illustrated comic books. Coal furnaces. Coal trucks. Coiled spring "snake" in a can. **Colonial Bread.** Continental kits. Cootie catchers. Crinolines. Crooners. Cufflinks. Curfew.

Dick Tracy. Diptheria. Dish night at the movie theatre. Dish towel premiums in soap powder boxes. Door-to-door mail delivery. Door-to-door photographers (with a live pony to pose on), door-to-door salesmen. Door-to-door surveys. Double features. Dusting chalkboard erasers. Duz soap powder.

Elevator operators. Ethyl (leaded) gasoline.

Fake bloody thumbs. Fake dog poop. Fake vomit. Fender skirts. Fibber McGee. Fire alarm boxes (on selected street corners). Flash-bulbs. Flashcubes. Floorwalkers. Flypaper. Follow-the-bouncing-ball sing-alongs at the movies. French roll (hair style). Front fender-mounted spare tires. Front porches. Fuller Brush men. Full-service gas stations.

Garters. Girdles. Girls' gym suits (usu-ally blue). Gliders. Glo-color satin jackets. Goiters. Gold fish given as carnival game prizes. Good Friday church services. Good luck pieces (rabbit's feet, four-leaf clovers, lucky pennies, etc.). Gooseneck telephones.

Halloween masks made of starched linen. Hand buzzers. Hand fans. Hats. Hood orna-ments. Horn-rimmed glasses. Horse-drawn conveyances.

Ice boxes. Icemen. Indian-head pennies. Inkwells (in school desks). Inner tubes. Inter-missions at the movies. Interurban train cars. Ipana toothpaste.

Jacks. Jalopies. Jewel Tea salesmen. Joe Palooka.

Katzenjammer Kids. Kewpie dolls. Key chains. Kits chewy mini-caramels.

"Lead" (steel) pennies. Leon Errol short comedy films. Little Beaver. Little Lulu. Little Rascals. Luden's cough drops. Lux bar soap.

Mandarin-collar shirts. Marbles. March of Dimes (with real dimes laid out on downtown sidewalk). Measles (a.k.a. Rubeola). Mexican jumping beans. Milkboxes. Milkmen. Mood rings. Moon discs (smooth hubcaps). Morning milk (served in grade school with one Graham cracker and one saltine cracker). Mouton coats. Movie theater ushers. Mumps.

Nuns in ankle-length robes and unusual headgear. Nurses in white uniforms with caps.

Oleo in a bag. **Omar Bread.** Ooga horns. Ozzie & Harriet.

Paddy wagons (a.k.a. "Black Marias"). Parakeets. Peacoats. Pea shooters. Penny candies. Penny loafers. Penny post cards. Pet chameleons (fastened to clothing with tiny gold chain). Pet Rocks. Pig tails. Pinch-nose glasses. Pocket handkerchiefs. Pocket watches. Pogo sticks. Polio. Poodle skirts. Polaroid cameras. Pony tails. Porch swings. Poultices. Poultry stores. Princess phone. Punch cards (I.B.M.). Pushcart vendors. Push-type lawnmowers.

Rabbit-ear TV antennaes. Rationing stamps (during WWII). Red Ryder. Revivals. Rotary dial telephones. Rubella (a.k.a. Roseola or German measles). Rug beaters. Running boards.

S & H Green Stamps. Sailor hats. Saturday serials. School satchels. Sea Monkeys. Senior cords. Sgt. Preston. Scrap drives (during WWII). Shirley Temple. Shirts made in America. Shoe horns. Shoe repair shops. Shoe stretchers. Shoeshine boys. Shoes made in America. Shrunken heads (fake). Singing cowboys. Sin-Sin breath freshener. Skate keys. Sky King. Slide rules. Smilin' Ed McConnell. Smith Brother's cough drops. Spare tires (full-size). Speedy Alka-Seltzer. Spotlights (on cars). Stewardesses. Stilts. Station wagons with real wood sides. Storybook dolls. Streetcars. Super Circus. Sweetheart bar soap.

Tail fins. Taking out the ashes. Tasselled shoestrings. Teel dentifrice. Tent meetings. Terry and the Pirates. The Great Gildersleeve. The Shadow. The Three Stooges. Tie clasps.

Tonettes. Tooth powder. Top Value Stamps. Tossle-head dolls. Trackless trolleys. Travelogs. Trolls (small dolls). Truth books. TV repairmen (that made house calls).

Uncle Wiggley.

Vacuum tube lines in department stores (that took money up to the office and returned your change and receipt). V.B.S. that lasted two weeks. Vests.

"Walking" toys (no batteries required). Wallpaper cleaner. Wax lips. Wax teeth. White gloves. Whooping cough. Womens' hats with veils. W.O.W. (patent medicine). Wringer-type washing machines.

X-ray machines in shoe stores.

Yellow fog lights. Yo-yos.

1 or 2-digit postal zones. 3-cent stamps. 3-night viewing in funeral homes. 3-piece mens' suits. 3-ring circuses in tents. 6-character phone numbers (example: FRanklin 6946). 6-ounce Cokes (for a nickel). 8-track tapes. 10-cent comic books. 33-rpm LP (long-play records. 35-cent paperback books. 45-rpm single-play records.

Appendix E

Common Things Today That Were Not Around While I Was Growing Up

Here's a collection of common things to-day that I never heard of while growing up in Indianapolis during the 1940s and most of the '50s. The main reason I never heard of many of them — at least not until after high school or later in my life — was because they had not yet been created, discovered, established, or invented. While some of these things may have existed elsewhere in the world at large, they did not exist in the world of my knowledge or experience. Underlined words existed during my childhood, but had totally different meanings back then.

A.A.R.P. A.B.S. Acid rain. Acid reflux. Adjustable beds. AIDS. Alkaline. All-beef. All-you-can-eat. Altoids. Aluminum ball bats. Amazon.com. Apps. Area codes. A.R.M.s. Ar-tificial Christmas trees. Artificial insemination. Asteroids. A.T.F. A.T.M. A.T.V. Automatic deposit. Automatic elevators. Automatic trans-missions.

Backpacks. Ball-points. Barbie dolls. Barcodes. Bariatric. Baskin-Robbins. Battery-powered. Ben & Jerry. Berber carpet. Big Mac. Bilingual signage. Birth-control pills. Blackberry. Black holes. Blizzard. Blockbuster. Blogs. Blue-Ray. Boogie boards. Boomboxes. Botox. Bratz. Breast implants. Buffalo wings. Bullet trains. Bungee jumping. Burger King. Burritoes. Bypass surgery.

Cable. CAD-CAM. Caffeine-free. Calculators. Cappuccino. Cargo pants. Carpal tunnel. Cartridge. Cassettes. CAT scan. CB radio. C.D.s. Cell phones. Center brake lights. Chemo. Chia Pets. Child-proof. Chip dip. Cholesterol. Chopper. Class action. Clones. Coke. Color television. .Coms. Contact lenses. Copiers. Crack. Credit cards. Crock Pots. Crocs. Cross trainers. Crunchy peanut butter. Curly fries.

Darth Vader. D.E.A. Death Star. Debit cards. Decaf. Defibrillators. Diet drinks. Digital. Ding-Dongs. Disposable diapers. Disposable lighters. Dish. Dishwasher. DNA. DOCKERS. Domed stadiums. Donkey-Kong. Dora the Explorer. Double-Stuf Oreos. Dreadlocks.

Drive-by shootings. Drive-up window. Dr. Oz. Dr. Phil. Dr. Seuss. Dumpsters. D.V.D.s. D.V.R.s.

Ear buds. Egg Beaters. Electric pencil sharpeners. Electric scissors. Electric screwdrivers. Electric staplers. *Electric typewriters.* Electronic keyboards. E-mail. E.M.T.s. Endoscopic surgery. E.P.A. E.S.L classes. ESPN. Extra crispy. Extra virgin. Eyeglasses in an hour.

Facebook. Fannie Mae. Fanny packs. Faux fur. Fax machines. FED-EX. Felt-tip markers. FEMA. Fiberglas. Flavored potato chips. Flip-flops. Fluoride toothpaste. Flu shots. FM radio. Foam mattresses. Free-range. Freddie Mac. Fun size. FX.

Game cube. Gap. Garbage disposals. Gasahol. Gas grills. Gay rights. Generic. George Foreman Grill. Ginsu Knife. Global warming. Golf carts. Google. Gore-Tex. G.P.S. Graffiti. Granola.

Haagen-Daz. Halogen. Hands-free. Hang gliding. Hard core. Hard Rock Cafe. Hardware. Headsets. Heat pumps. Hepatitis-B. HEPA filters. Hibachis. Hi-Fi. High def.

Holograms. HOME DEPOT. Homogenized.
Hoodies. Hooters. Hot Pockets. Hottie. Hot
tubs. Huff. Humvees.

I.C.B.M.s. Icon. Identity theft. I.E.D.
IHOP. Inkjets. I.N.S. Instant coffee. Instant
Jello. Instant tea. Internet. Interstate highways.
Intraocular lenses (for cataract patients). In-
vitro fertilization. IPOD. I.R.A .s.

Jacuzzi. Jet planes. Jet skis. Jogging.
Joint-replacement surgery. Jumbotron.

Keno. Kevlar. K.F.C. Kiddie porn. Kilo.
Kilometer. King-size. Kiosk. Krispy-Creme.
Kung fu.

Lap bands. Lap dances. Laptops. Lasers.
Lasik. Latex paint. Latte. L'eggs. Lego. L.E.D.s.
L.E.M. Lemon-pepper. Lexan. Light saber.
Lipitor. Liquid detergents. Lite. Liter. Little
Debbie. Low-fat. Lotto. Lowe's. Low-sodium.
L.S.D. Luke Skywalker.

Mace. Macro-biotics. MADD. Madonna.
Mag-Lite. Mag wheels. Mall. Mammograms.
McDonald's. Melanoma. Meth. Micro brew-
ery. Micro chips. Microwaves. Moonies.

<u>Mouse</u>. Mousepads. Mr. Coffee. M.R.E.s. M.R.I.s. Mr. T. Mullet. Muppets.

Nail guns. Narc. NASA. Neonatal. Nerf. Nikes. No-line bifocals. Nordic Track. Nuclear power.

Old Navy. One-size-fits-all socks. Open-heart surgery. Oprah. Organ transplants. Organic. OSHA. <u>Outback</u>. Ozone layer.

Pacemakers. Pac-Man. Paintball. Palm Pilot. Pantyhose. Paper shredders. Patch-dispensed medications. Pay-per-view. P.C.s. People movers. Piercings (except for ears). Pilates. Pixel. Pizza. Pizza Hut. Polar fleece. Polarized sunglasses. *Polaroid cameras*. Polyester. Polyethylene. Polypropylene. Polyurethane. Pop Tarts. Post-It notes. Power brakes. Power steering. Power windows. Prepackaged lunch meat. Pringles. Pull-tab cans. P.V.C.

Quarter-pounder. Queen-size. Q.V.C.

Radial tires. Ragu. Rainbow Coalition. Ranch dressing. Rear-window defogger. <u>Recall</u>. Recession. Recycle. Red Lobster. Relo (relocation). <u>Remote</u>. Reno (renovation). Rent-

To-Own. Roadies. Robocop. Robotics. ROGAINE. Roller blades. R-rated. Rubik's Cube.

Saddle blocks. Safflower oil. Salad bars. Salsa. Sam's Club. Saran-Wrap. Satellites. Scanners. Scooby-Doo. Scrabble. Seat belts. Segues. Self-adhesive postage stamps. Self-serve. Seniors. Sexual harassment. Shar-Pei. Shih Tzu. Shinsplints. Shopaholics. Shopping centers. Silicone. SIRIUS radio. Skateboards. Skin art. Skittles. Sky diving. Slim-Fast. Smog. Smoke detectors. Snort. Soccer. Software. So-lar- powered. Space shuttle. Spandex. Speedos. Spin doctors. Spongebob Squarepants. Spray-cans. Staples. Starbuck's. Star Trek. Star Wars. S.T.Ds. Stem cells. Stents. Stereos. Steroids. Strobe lights. Styrofoam. Substance abuse. Subway. Sudoku. Sugar-free. Super Bowl. Super glue. Supersize. Surveillance cameras. Sushi. S.U.V.s. SWAT teams. Synthesizers.

Tacos. Taco Bell. Tamper-resistant. Tan-ning beds. Target. Tasers. Teenage Mutant Ninja Turtles. Temp. Terminal. Terminator. Terrorism. Terrorists. The Simpsons. Thinsulate. Thongs. Time-release. Tinted win-dows. T.M. Touch-screens. Touch-tone. Toner.

Trackballs. Trail mix. Tree huggers. Trivial Pursuit. Tubeless tires. TV trays. Twitter. Twizzlers. Tylenol.

Ugli (citrus fruit). U-Haul. U.P.S. Ultra-sounds. Ultrasuede. Unleaded. U.V. Uzi.

Vanity plates. Variable-speed wipers. V.C.R.s. Verizon. Vertical blinds. Viagra. Video games. Vinyl siding. Virtual reality.

Waffle cones. WAL-MART. Water beds. <u>Web</u>. Weight Watchers. Whiteboards. WI-FI. Wii. Wine in a box. <u>Wireless</u>. Wookie. World Wide Web. W.W.J.D.

X-Box. Xerox. X Files. X-Men. XM Radio.

<u>Yahoo</u>! Yoga. Yogurt. You Tube.

ZIP codes. Zip-Lock. Zip ties.

4-wheelers. 6-packs. 18-wheelers. .357-Magnum. 38 ice cream flavors. 9-1-1.

Appendix F

Do You Remember?

This is a list of places that were in the Wright Street neighborhood during the 1940s and '50s. This area stretched from Buchanan Street down to Raymond Street and from S. East Street over to Shelby Street. The Fountain Square area, Garfield Park, uptown, and other adjacent areas are also included in separate groupings, as well as a few scary places around town. Some of these places remain today and are basically unchanged. A few remain but have been remodeled and/or repurposed. Several have been closed and/or torn down. A couple of special categories have been thrown in just for fun. If you lived back then, see how many you can still remember. Names shown in boldface type are mentioned in this book.

Wright Street neighborhood
Abraham Lincoln School #18. American Can Co. Bemis Bag Co. Blue Ribbon Ice Cream Shop. Brande's Drug & Cigar Store. **City Sanitation Department garage and stables.** Cliff's Barber

Shop. **Dr. Charles Reid's office.** Emhardt Clinic. Fireside South Restaurant. **Fisher's Market.** Franklin Pure Milk & Ice Cream Co. G. H. Hermann Funeral Home. Gohmanan's Grocery (operated by Mr. & Mrs. Bonewits). Harry's Meat Market (a.k.a. Stein's Grocery). **Horace Mann School #13.** J. L. Holcomb Co. Joe's Coney Island. L. & H. Hardware. Larry's Tiny Diner. Lincoln Theater (the "Stinkin' Lincoln"). Newman's Market. **Nilges' Bakery.** Nine Star Tavern. Owen's Market. **Pantzer's Pharmacy.** Payne's Market. Ransberg's (painted metal products factory). Reiman's Florist Shop and greenhouses. Ringgold Playground. Sickel's TV Repair. Sinclair gas station. Spreen's Market. St. John's E. & R. Church. Stokes' Pharmacy. St. Paul's Lutheran School. Stokely-Van Camp canning factory. Sugar Bowl. Trinity Evangelical Danish Lutheran Church (held Weekday Religious Education classes for School #13 students). Troub Memorial Church. **Weddle's Drug Store.**

Fountain Square area
A & P Supermarket. **Ace Leather & Hobby Shop.** Ban-Dee Restaurant & Cocktail Lounge. **City Sanitation Department garage and stables.** Danner's Dime Store. Fountain Square

Bowling Alley (duckpins). Fountain Square Poultry Market. **Fountain Square Record Shop.** Fountain Square Theatre. G.C. Murphy Five & Dime Store. Granada Theater. Greasy Spoon Cafe. Gulf gas station. Hoeping's Hardware. Hook's Drug Store. **Indianapolis News District Substation.** J. C. Wilson Funeral Home. John's Lunch. Langsenkamp-Wheeler Brassworks. Merchants' Bank. Merit's Shoe Store. Miles' Grocery. Pacific Finance. Pedigo Jewelers. Peppy Grill. Sanders Theater. Schiff Shoes. Shelby Furniture. Skip's Market. Smitty's Diner (built inside an old streetcar or interurban car). Steve's Chili Parlor. St. Patrick's Catholic Church and school. Teamsters' Union Hall. The Coffee Cup. Thomann's Shoe Store. Thunderbird Tavern. Tom & Art's Barbershop. Wade's Drug Store.

Garfield Park
Amphitheater. Civil War Memorial. Conservatory. Garfield's statue. Greenhouse. Humpback bridge ("Tickle-Belly Bridge"). Pagoda ("The Pavilion"). Shelter House. Sledding hill ("Raymond Street Hill"). Swimming pool. Sunken Gardens. Tennis courts. The Lagoon (winter ice skating area where Bean Creek and Pleasant Run join).

Adrian's Orchards. Avalon Theater. Bear &
Bull Tavern. Berringer's Tavern. Blue Point.
Buck's Supermarket. Buescher Florists. Burgoo
Lunch. Carnival grounds (Southern and Madi-
son Avenues). Carlos Bakery. City Ice & Fuel
Co. Columbia Park. Coppi's Drug Store. Darko
& Sons Cleaners. Delavan Smith Athletic Field.
Dog & Suds. Eli Lilly & Co. Emrich's Furniture
Store. Ernie Pyle V.F.W. Post. Fox Roller Skat-
ing Rink. Garfield Theater ("The Dink"). Gee's
Drugs. German Park. Gregg's Laundry & Dry
Cleaning. Harry E. Wood High School.
Hawkins Drugs. Indianapolis Statuary Co.
(made plaster carnival figurines). J.H. Taylor
Moving & Storage. Key West Shrimp House.
Longacre Park and pool. Madison Avenue
Flower Shop. Manual High School (old).
Manual High School (new). Maria's Pizza.
Merrill Street underpass. Michael's Drug Store
(2 locations). Morgan's Restaurant. National
Guard Armory. Oriental Theater. Pasquale's
Pizza. Pittman-Moore Pharmaceutical Com-
pany. **Polar Ice & Fuel Co.** Prospect Branch
Library. Rader's Shell Station. Reagan's Bak-
ery. Red Dot Potato Chip factory. Sacred Heart
High School. Schuster's Block Co. Shapiro's
Delicatessen. Shelby Street Savings and Loan.

Southern Circle Restaurant. Southport High School. Southside Farmers' Market. South Side Turners (a.k.a., Turner's Athenaeum). Southwind Restaurant. Sport Bowl. Standard Oil Station. Stop & Shop Supermarket. Stout Field. Studebaker Realty Co. **Tee Pee Restaurant** (southside). Twin Drive-in Theater.

Uptown (Mile Square)
Alamo Theater (westerns). Banner-Whitehill Furniture Store. Bus Station (Traction Terminal Building). Cadle Tabernacle. Children's Museum. Circle Theater. Claypool Hotel. Columbia Club. Cottage Restaurant. Craig's (famous for "Persian Nut Sundaes"). DeBiase's Italian Restaurant. Downey Dunker Donut Shop. English Theater. Esquire Theater. Fendrick's Restaurant. Fox Theater (burlesque). John Herron Art Institute & Museum. Harry Levinson's. Indiana Theater. Jap Jones' Bar & Restaurant. Keith's Theater. Kreig's Catholic Supply Store. Loew's Theater. L. S. Ayres' Department Store. L. Stauss & Co. Lyric Theater. Merchant's Bank & Trust Co. Military Park. Monument Circle. Morris Plan Building. Morrow's Nut House. Murat Temple. Mutual Theater (burlesque). **Outdoor wrestling arena.** P. H. Hulskamp Saw Sharpening. Power &

Light Building. Railway Express Agency. Rodeo Theater (westerns). Russett's Cafeteria. Scottish Rite Cathedral. Soldiers and Sailors Monument. S. S. Kresge's. State Capitol Building. Stationer's. St. Elmo's Steak House. Three Sisters. Toddle House. Union Station. H. P. Wasson's Department Store. University Park. Walker Theater. Water Company Canal. Weiss' Delicatessen. William H. Block Co. Department Store. World War Memorial. YMCA.

Other areas around town
Al Green's Drive-In Restaurant and Theater. Allison Division of General Motors. Art Zipp's Speedway. Bell-Air Drive-In Theater. Butler Fieldhouse. Central State Hospital. Chevrolet Plant. Coliseum. Diamond Chain Co. Greenwood Drive-In Theater. Haag's Drugs. Indiana State Fairgrounds. Indianapolis Motor Speedway (Home of the 500). International Harvester. Kingan & Co. Knobby's (2 locations). Marrott Hotel. Maywood Drive-In Theater. Milano Inn. Pendleton Pike Drive-In Theater. Plainfield Boy's School. Riverside Amusement Park and Roller Rink. Roslyn Bakeries. Royster Fertilizer Plant. Rustic Gardens. Shadeland Drive-In Theater. Sixteenth Street Speedway (midget and stock car race track). Stark &

Wetzel. Stockyards. Stout Field. Tee Pee Restaurant (northside). The Pole. Tibbs Drive-In Theater. Victory Field. Weir Cook Airport. Westlake Drive-In Theater and Swimming Pool.

Scary locations in and around town
Crown Hill Cemetary/38th Street (ghostly woman reportedly seen on rainy nights walking alone along 38th Street, people stopping to give her a ride are amazed when she disappears and leaves a wet spot on the seat where she had been sitting). Haunted Bridge at Avon (you could sometimes hear eerie screams from ghost of a girl or a couple who jumped or fell to their death, or the workman who fell into the concrete when the bridge was being built and was sealed inside forever). Haunted House on South Meridian Street (exact location was never determined). House of Blue Lights (where a woman's preserved body was kept in a glass-topped coffin by her grieving husband in a big old house illuminated by eerie blue lights and surrounded by a high fence guarded by Dobermans, or German Shepherds, or even by a bear as one version claims).

Radio stations
WGEE ("Wee-Gee"), WIBC, WIRE, WISH, WXLW.

Radio disc jockeys
"Bouncing Bill" Baker ("The Music Maker").
Easy Gwinn ("The Happy Medium that Every-
one Wants to Strike;" he also had The Rabbit's
Club).

Appendix G

Southside Indianapolis Trivia

Here are some interesting facts discovered while doing research for this book. See how many you knew.

The Citizens Street Railway Company once ran mule-drawn streetcars out Virginia Avenue as far as the intersection of Prospect and Shelby Streets. A streetcar turnaround was located at this intersection in what became Fountain Square. The surrounding area was originally known as "The End" by local residents because the streetcar line ended there.

There once was an actual fountain in Fountain Square used to water horses and mules. It was called the Subscription Fountain because it was built by money raised through subscribers who donated money to support the project.

Two different statues have been located atop the fountain in Fountain Square over the years.

The first statue was called the Lady of the Fountain. It was toppled in 1919 when a local merchant strung a rope to it to support a large banner advertising a sale at his store. A strong wind blowing on the banner toppled the statue and it was destroyed.

The second statue was called the Pioneer Family and was erected in 1924.

This fountain and statue was removed to Garfield Park in 1954 and returned to Fountain Square in 1969.

The original St. Patrick's Catholic Church was burned down by an arsonist in 1927. The existing church building is the *second* one built on the site.

At one time during the early 1900s there were almost a dozen movie theaters in and around the Fountain Square area and it became known as the city's theater district.

These theaters included the Apollo, Arcade, Arcadia, Bair, Eagle, Elite, Imperial, Iris, Laurel, Sanders Apex (later reopened as the Sanders), and Star. All these were closed by the 1920s.

In addition to these indoor theaters, several "outdoor" theaters were operated on vacant lots during the summer months. These included the Elm Airdome, Fountain Airdome, Garfield Airdome, Green's Open Air, and Virginia Airdome.

The Fountain Square commercial district is listed on the National Register of Historic Places.

During the late 1800s and early 1900s, many of the streets in the Wright Street-Fountain Square neighborhood had other names than those familiar to area residents in the 1940s and '50s:
- Cottage Avenue east of Shelby Street was once called Willow Street.
- Leonard Street was originally known as McKeanan or McKernan Street.
- Noble Street was formerly Beaty Street.
- Orange Street was once called Downey Street and prior to that, the portion east of S. East was known as Birkenmayer Street.
- Parkway Avenue was originally called Dunlop Street.
- Prospect Street between S. East and Shelby was once named Coburn Street.
- Sanders Street was once called Yeiser Street.

- Shelby Street was formerly Dillon Street.
- St. Patrick Street was at one time called Hunter Street and before that it was known as Short Street.
- Terrace Avenue was originally named Nebraska Street.
- Woodlawn Avenue was once called Dougherty Street. The one-block section angling northeast from Virginia Avenue over to Shelby was once known as Elk Street.
- Wright Street from E. McCarty down to Buchanan was at one time called Sullivan Street.

Calvin Fletcher School #8 was named for the head of the first family to settle in the area later known as Fountain Square. He and his partner Nicholas McCarty was instrumental in converting the area from farmland into town lots.

Horace Mann School #13 was named for the famous American educator (1796-1859) and is listed on the National Register of Historic Places.

Abraham Lincoln School #18 was built on a site that had been occupied by a band of Delaware Indians until 1820.

The brick house across Palmer Street from

School #18 (the one that sits back at an odd angle to the street) was built in 1828 and is the oldest surviving brick house in Marion County.

The infamous James W. "Jim" Jones (leader of the religious cult that committed mass suicide at their compound in Jonestown, Guyana) had his *first* ministry as an associate pastor at the Laurel Street Tabernacle. He imported and sold monkeys from South America to raise money for the church.

Dale Mortenbeck (School #13, School #8, Manual Class of 1956) ended up getting one of those monkeys from its original buyer. Dale named him Zippy (he lived for twenty-two years). On summer days, Wright Street-Fountain Square area kids might remember seeing Zippy in Dale's backyard at the southwest corner of Prospect and Leonard.

Ever remember seeing an airplane (minus the wings) parked beside a house somewhere in the Wright Street-Fountain Square neighborhood? Guesswhere it was? In Dale Mortenbeck's side yard. His dad bought the wrecked 1946 Aircoupe and eventually restored it. At one time or another he also had several other aircraft in the yard along with other unusual items.

John Dillinger, the notorious bank robber of the 1930s, reportedly used to get his hair cut at a barber shop on the west side of Shelby Street just north of Troy Avenue.

David Dampier (Manual Class of 1956) says his father (now deceased) told him about an undocumented incident from the 1930s involving Dillinger and some of his gang members being at the home/office of a Dr. E. E. Rose at 2153 Barth Avenue. The cops found out about it, raided the place, and a shootout ensued. One cop was wounded (killed?) and the gang got away. Nothing about this was ever published in the local newspapers.

The girl who sat on top of the pole at the Southwind Restaurant on Shelby Street for several months as an advertising stunt was named Mauri (Rose) Kirby. She was once a student at Manual High School (not a graduate).

Red Dot Potato Chips, a popular local brand, were produced in a factory on the west side of Madison Avenue just south of the old Belt R.R. tracks. This company was purchased by and absorbed into the Frito-Lay Corporation. The original building is still standing and in use as a warehouse. Garfield Park was originally called the Southern Driving Park.

The owners of the Southern Circle Restaurant also operated another drive-in restaurant called the Southern Triangle. It was located out Highway #67 on the southwest side, but never flourished like the Circle. Eventually it changed hands and was renamed the Maywood Drive-In Restaurant.

Made in the USA
Middletown, DE
12 November 2018